ADVANCE PRAISE

"Anyone who knows Dhoruba Bin Wahad knows he is never at a loss for words. And so it is that in this age of reactionary politics, revisionist, and opportunist narratives lining the pockets of those beneficiaries of corporate book deals, paid activism, nonprofit funding, social media and mainstream accolades, this collection of his writings couldn't come at a better time. For seven decades and counting, Dhoruba's life has been one of stiff resistance, love for the people, and insightful analysis." —**dequi kioni-sadiki**, Black Panther Collective member, former chair of Malcolm X Commemoration, Spirit of Mandela Coordinating Committee member, Northeast Political Prisoner Coalition

"Black Panther Party members have similarities in their pre-party backgrounds, but never the same story. I was a recruiter for the BPP in the Bronx, where Dhoruba and I are both from, back in 1968, but I didn't meet him until years later in the Southern District federal lockdown in November 1982. The truth remains: Dhoruba was solid then and he is solid now." —**Bilal Sunni Ali**, veteran Black Panther, saxophonist with Gil Scott-Heron's Midnight Band

"True to his name, Dhoruba Bin Wahad is a human being made of lightning and thunder. He was the very first Black revolutionary that I met with who really talked it, and walked it, to tell it. He took it and still shook it. His razor tongue is backed by laser wit. Still, all these years on, he is a strategist teaching us how to move on the chessboard of this ongoing struggle. Pick up *Revolution in These Times* and keep it moving." —**Chuck D**, Public Enemy

"Dhoruba Bin Wahad is a towering figure in the Black freedom struggle for the past five decades! His love for Black people and courage to serve and sacrifice for Black freedom are legendary! Don't miss this monumental book!" —**Dr. Cornel West**

"*Revolution in These Times* is an invaluable resource for anyone interested in reading the analyses of those silenced by mainstream media" —**Robert J. Boyle**, attorney for Dhoruba Bin Wahad

"All that you want to know more deeply about the wisdoms and lessons of the Black Panther Party and Black Liberation Army will be here in this book, in the words of someone who was intimately familiar with its core ideology and practice. Years in prison did not dim his light nor douse his fire. What Dhoruba Bin Wahad courageously shares is given freely and with blunt warning for those who take on or stay on the path of revolution without blinders. My own entry into the membership of the BPP and ranks of the BLA recognized his brilliance and dedication to the 'Power to the People' in building the United Front 'by any means necessary.' I am still in awe of his lumpen brilliance. A must read!" —**Ashanti Omowali Alston**, anarchist writer and activist, former member of the Black Panther Party and Black Liberation Army

"Dhoruba's voice is timeless and much needed in an era where Black voices are marginalized and, in many cases, criminalized. His lessons are critical in providing a historical framework of Black nationalism and encouraging control over our economic and political destinies. As a former member of the Black Panther Party and leader of the Black Liberation Army, Dhoruba is instrumental in teaching readers about the failed policies of the past and the importance of self-determination for the future." —**Teri Thompson**, attorney for Mutulu Shakur and Kamau Sadiki

"Dhoruba Bin Wahad's analysis is hard hitting, uncompromising, and forward focused. This book is an ideological weapon to cut through the fog of lies and propaganda perpetuated by capitalism and imperialism, helping us plot a course to a revolutionary future." —**Eugene Puryear**, journalist, *Breakthrough News*

"*Revolution in These Times* should be required reading for young people to understand our struggle. Political education is needed more now than ever considering the time we live in. Educate to liberate." —**Yasmeen Majid**, veteran Black Panther

"My comrade Dhoruba Bin Wahad is an organic authentic revolutionary whose analysis is 'right on time' for these twenty-first century revolutionary times! Keep speaking truth to power, Brother Dhoruba, you paid enough dues! Our victory is certain!" —**Charles Barron**, founding member Operation Power, veteran Black Panther, former member of NYC Council and former member of NYS Assembly

"In these conversations Dhoruba Bin Wahad proves that the liberation movement still lives. His work and his experience are inspirations and a blueprint for us to act upon." —**Margaret Kimberley**, *Black Agenda Report*

"*Revolution in These Times* is not just a book, it's a blueprint for Black liberation. Dhoruba Bin Wahad confronts the harsh realities of systemic oppression and lays out a path toward true freedom and self-determination. Wahad's words are a powerful reminder that our struggle is far from over and that revolutionary change is necessary to dismantle the forces of white supremacy." —**Rahiem Shabazz**, award-winning filmmaker and journalist

"The perspective of Dhoruba Bin Wahad remains a valuable strategy as we continue the revolution for liberation." —**Malik Ismail**, author of *From Old Guard to Vanguard: A Second Generation Panther* and host of *The Vanguard Show*

"Dhoruba Bin Wahad is a revolutionary for every era. Wahad's work, analysis, and reflections bear a timeless quality and acute relevance to the present. *Revolution in These Times* is a powerful, indelible proclamation, and guide in the resistance against fascism and the forging of a united front against repression. This publication represents a victory over the machinations of empire which seek to erase warriors like Wahad. Indeed, the text and the enduring example of Wahad urges us to remember: 'We will not give up the fight.'" —**Jenipher Jones**, attorney for Leonard Peltier

"Since his release from prison in the early 1990s, Dhoruba Bin Wahad has been an inspiration to generations of young activists and organizers. This former Black Panther and nineteen-year political prisoner continues to provide a revolutionary and insurgent analysis that offers a radical way forward in the current era of global genocide and the duopoly of domestic repression." —**TJ Whitaker**, New Jersey teacher, organizer, and cofounder of MapSO Freedom School

"Even as more Black Panther veterans are getting a little more media attention, the words and wisdom of Dhoruba Bin Wahad are especially unique, poignant, and profound. Well beyond his own experiences as an organizer, political prisoner, and educator, his international analysis as a Pan-Africanist are unparalleled and need to be carefully read—by academics and activists alike." —**Matt Meyer**, Secretary-General, International Peace Research Association

"One thing about Dhoruba, he is going to make it plain. He's direct, yet thorough, and mindful of the varying levels of knowledge within the room, ensuring the audience can walk away with a solid understanding of his position. In the age of rampant misinformation and Al personification, going directly to the source is top-tier knowledge acquisition. Get you some." —**Sajdah Asmau**, Public Voices Fellow, National Black Child Development Institute

"Dhoruba Bin Wahad is more than merely a pragmatist; he is a pivotal figure that stands among other notable African world figures who, without hesitation, risked everything to achieve liberation by any means necessary. His writings, interviews, and foresight reflect his activism, dedication, and deep involvement in the movement's actions." —**Cimarron Reed-Bandele**, Marcus Garvey Society

"Dhoruba Bin Wahad is that truth-spitting OG mentor who happens to double as a living legend. His consistency and tenacious approach for our people stretches well beyond five decades of service, despite personal pains, trials and tribulations. This level of dedication and commitment highlights the profound fact that true revolutionaries who continuously fight on behalf of Black liberation must learn to love us, more than we hate ourselves." —**Marcus Coleman**, Save OurSelves founder and Fulton County Reparations Taskforce founding member, Vice Chair

REVOLUTION IN THESE TIMES

REVOLUTION IN THESE TIMES

Black Panther Party Veteran Dhoruba Bin Wahad on Antifascism, Black Liberation, and a Culture of Resistance

Dhoruba Bin Wahad
Edited by Kalonji Jama Changa
Introduction by Joy James

Brooklyn, NY
Philadelphia, PA
commonnotions.org

Revolution in These Times
Black Panther Party Veteran Dhoruba Bin Wahad
on Antifascism, Black Liberation, and a Culture of Resistance

Edited and with a preface by Kalonji Jama Changa
Introduction by Joy James
Afterword by Bibi Olugbala Angola

The conversations in this book are edited and abridged versions of a series of interviews conducted for Black Power Media.

ISBN: 978-1-945335-13-6 | eBook ISBN: 978-1-945335-41-9
Library of Congress Number: 2024950695

10 9 8 7 6 5 4 3 2 1

Common Notions
c/o Interference Archive
314 7th St.
Brooklyn, NY 11215

Common Notions
c/o Making Worlds Bookstore
210 S. 45th St.
Philadelphia, PA 19104

www.commonnotions.org
info@commonnotions.org

Discounted bulk quantities of our books are available for organizing, educational, or fundraising purposes. Please contact Common Notions at the address above for more information.

Cover design by Josh MacPhee
Layout design and typesetting by Sydney Rainer
Printed by union labor in Canada on acid-free paper

CONTENTS

DEDICATION

Revolution in These Times is dedicated to the courageous members of the Black Panther Party, the Black Liberation Army, the Student Nonviolent Coordinating Committee, the Revolutionary Action Movement, the Black Guerrilla Family, the Black August Organizing Committee, and the Jericho Movement. Your unwavering dedication to the struggle for justice, equality, and liberation has paved the way for future generations in the fight against oppression.

To the FTP Movement and all those who continue to challenge this violent system of oppression: your commitment to the cause of liberation inspires us all to remain steadfast in our pursuit of justice.

To our ancestors, whose sacrifices and wisdom have guided us: we honor your legacy and the foundation you have laid for the ongoing struggle for freedom.

To Dhoruba's sons, Mumu and Saif, his entire family, and comrades: I dedicate this work to you for sharing his energy and love with the rest of us. Your support and commitment to preserving his legacy remind us of the enduring power of community and the bonds that unite us in our shared pursuit of justice.

To my family: I acknowledge my absence when you may have needed me most. Your love and support have been my foundation, and I am grateful for your understanding and patience. I vow to spend the rest of my time on this planet correcting wrongs and perfecting imperfections.

And to the future freedom fighters: may your voices ring out with the strength of those who came before you. May you carry the torch of revolution into the future, ever committed to the ideals of justice, equality, and liberation for all. In solidarity and gratitude, we dedicate this work to you.

To the readers: get on the right side of the barricades, fight for the liberation of our political prisoners, and call for the end of this corrupt, criminal, and rotten system.

Ready for revolution!

ACKNOWLEDGMENTS

I want to express my deepest gratitude to all those who have contributed to the development and completion of this book on the thoughts of Dhoruba Bin Wahad, a remarkable figure whose life and activism have left an indelible mark on the struggle for justice and equality in the US and abroad.

First and foremost, I would like to thank Dhoruba Bin Wahad for his willingness to share his insights, stories, and experiences. His courage and resilience in the face of adversity are legendary, and his commitment to social justice and human rights has greatly inspired my work and many others. Thank you to Dr. Joy James, whose idea sparked the energy to transform the numerous video interviews into this book, *Revolution in These Times*. I am grateful to Black Power Media, the FTP Movement, scholars, and activists who provided their invaluable knowledge and perspective on the Black Panther Party, the Black Liberation Army, and the broader human and civil rights movement. Your research and writings have helped shape the contextual framework necessary for understanding Dhoruba's impact and the significance of his work.

To the editors and publishing team at Common Notions: thank you for your expertise, patience, and unwavering support throughout this process. Your guidance has been crucial in refining my thoughts and ensuring that Dhoruba's story is told with clarity and respect.

A heartfelt thanks to my family, friends, and comrades for their encouragement and understanding during the long hours spent researching and writing. Your belief in the importance of this project has kept me motivated and focused.

Lastly, I would like to acknowledge all the unsung heroes of the Black Liberation Movement who fought tirelessly for justice. Their efforts continue to inspire generations and remind us all of the vital importance of standing up for what is right.

Revolutionary Love!

PREFACE

THE STORM AND THE WHIRLWIND

Five decades ago, the legendary poet, singer, and cultural worker Gil Scott-Heron defiantly penned the liberation classic, "The Revolution Will Not Be Televised." Today, some may look at the play-by-play, in-your-face Palestinian genocide broadcast through social media and various forms of mercenary media globally and think that Scott-Heron miscalculated. Brother Gil was so on point that the message still confuses the pretentious spectators critiquing the players as they lounge comfortably in their living rooms across the empire.

In May 1971, the same year that Gil Scott-Heron gifted the world with "The Revolution Will Not Be Televised," Thomas Curry and Nicholas Binetti, two uniformed New York City police officers, who were guarding the home of Manhattan district attorney Frank S. Hogan, were shot repeatedly with a .45 caliber machine gun. The cops, although seriously wounded, survived the shooting, and prominent NY Black Panther Party Field Secretary and Black Liberation Army cofounder Dhoruba Bin Wahad was charged and sentenced to twenty-five years to life.

As readers will learn from the following pages of this book, Dhoruba Bin Wahad would go on to serve nineteen years in prison before the federal government would acknowledge and admit that he was a target of the Federal Bureau of Investigations' COINTELPRO. Upon his release, Wahad hit the ground running and continued to fight for the liberation of other political prisoners and the human rights of colonized and oppressed people worldwide.

Revolution in These Times: Black Panther Party Veteran Dhoruba Bin Wahad on Antifascism, Black Liberation, and a Culture of Resistance is personal to me because of the relationship I built with Dhoruba over the past two decades. Undoubtedly, Dhoruba is one of the most brilliant minds in both the Black Liberation Movement and freedom-fighting circles internationally. Although Dhoruba is one of my chief elders and OGs (original guerrillas) the camaraderie is more like that of an uncle or big brother. A combination of both comrade and family, to his sons, Mumu and Saif, I am "Uncle Kalonji."

The life and works of Dhoruba Bin Wahad should be taught, uplifted, and revered within the halls where revolution is studied and organized worldwide. It is with great honor that we introduce the works of a man whose name should be a common household word. Dhoruba is Swahili for "the Storm." Indeed, Dhoruba has lived up to his title and the world will know his name.

Revolutionary love to my brother, comrade, and friend, 'til we win!

—Kalonji Jama Changa

INTRODUCTION
REMEMBER THE PANTHER RESISTANCE

In late-1960s New York, where Dhoruba Bin Wahad was based as a Black Panther Party leader in Harlem, the Federal Bureau of Investigation and New York City police forces partnered to destroy the BPP in the now-infamous Panther 21 conspiracy trial. By bringing false charges against nearly two dozen members of the Black Panthers, the state, through malfeasance and mendacious lies, sought to destroy a political organization which was bringing food, decent housing, education, and medical care to oppressed and under-resourced communities.

The trial began in April 1969, and after eight months a New York City jury took only a few hours to acquit the defendants of all charges, including terrorism charges. Black radical activists had been railroaded by the state. The months or years in prison diminished their capacity to organize, work with, and provide for the people who needed care, protections, food and who also supported the Panthers.[1]

Later that year, COINTELPRO, the counterintelligence program of the FBI, in a joint task force with the Chicago Police Department (CPD) assassinated Fred Hampton and Mark Clark in a December 4 predawn raid. A week later, on December 11, the Los Angeles Police Department (LAPD) tried to exact a similar—but this time unsuccessful—killing of Panthers in Southern California

1 *Look for Me in the Whirlwind: From the Panther 21 to the 21st Century Revolutions*, coedited by dequi kioni-sadiki and Matt Meyer (Oakland: PM Press, 2017), analyzes the period of oppression and resistance, and includes Dhoruba Bin Wahad, Sekou Odinga, Jamal Joseph, Imam Jalil al Amin (formerly known as H. Rap Brown, imprisoned in Georgia; the Jericho Movement and In the Spirit of Mandela continue to advocate for his release).

by deploying a SWAT team, the first-ever special weapons and tactics drill and militarized hardware used in the United States. The CPD and LAPD predawn raids constituted a lethal legalized attack on people protesting poverty and racism, whose suffering and the violence meted out against them Hollywood would sensationalize and, in some ways, trivialize.

Dhoruba, though, had jumped bail and went underground; thus, he became ensnared in COINTELPRO machinations and ended up being incarcerated for nearly twenty years, framed for crimes he did not commit. Dhoruba and other Panther-aligned revolutionaries who evaded assassination became political prisoners. These revolutionaries were the "rainbow" resisters of which slain panther Fred Hampton spoke. Among them were white revolutionaries such as Laura Whitehorn, Marilyn Buck, Tom Manning, and Indigenous revolutionaries such as Leonard Peltier.[2]

The state's counterintelligence program destabilized organizations and liberation movements in the US and elsewhere to ensure that power remain consolidated with state and corporate and repressive nationalists who sought to control or capture those who wanted to live freely in a socially healthy and just environment. It is a blessing that Dhoruba Bin Wahad survived COINTELPRO and was able to share this brilliant book with us.

BOOKS WILL SHAPE YOUR LIFE

My first introduction to the Panthers was through a book. This is the norm for the vast majority of people who learned or are learning about the BPP without filters and distortions. It was 1987, years after the Black Panthers and the Black Liberation Army had been dismantled as revolutionary formations. Dhoruba Bin Wahad was a veteran of both formations, but I did not know his name back then, when I took the subway to West 125th Street to attend a book launch in Harlem at the Adam Clayton Powell State Office building. Black militant women, BPP veterans, had organized a

2 For more on the political prisoners and the history of state violence and repression, see the Jericho Movement, https://www.thejerichomovement.com, and *Imprisoned Intellectuals: America's Political Prisoners Write on Life, Liberation, and Rebellion*, ed. Joy James (London: Rowman & Littlefield, 2003).

book reading and promotional launch for *Assata Shakur: An Autobiography*. With irony and defiance, they hosted a book party for a woman who had been broken out of prison in 1979 by BLA leader Sekou Odinga (who would be imprisoned and tortured for over thirty years by the state for a freedom or emancipation endeavor in which no one was injured) and Italian citizen Sylvia Baraldini, who was incarcerated for twenty years in a US prison for assisting Assata Shakur to escape captivity.

I brought my copy home, which of course had no signature by the author, and began to teach my students Assata's memoir and other information on liberation struggles in the US by those seeking to vanquish enslavement, exploitation, poverty, and dishonor. Through one book, I became a student-teacher of freedom struggles. The content was challenging for semi-protected employees holding onto salary, medical care, and pension—and for students seeking the same. Gradually, we better understood the history of our struggle against enslavers and purchasers. There were connections and communities woven together in national and international struggles. Assata, Dhoruba's comrade from Harlem, was persecuted by the FBI, shot and tortured by New Jersey Troopers. She lost her comrade and bodyguard Zayd Shakur to gun fire or police crossfire that also led to the death of NJ Trooper Werner Forester. Attorney Leonard Hinds competently details that traumatic encounter (and the possibility that "friendly fire" killed Forester but not Zayd Shakur). Sundiata Acoli, who was driving the car with the three BLA members, briefly escaped but was captured and incarcerated for nearly fifty years until his release in 2022. Attorney Hinds details the facts of Shakur's innocence and how she was targeted for lethal repression by the state as its counter-revolutionary police forces drove committed rebels underground and then attempted to assassinate them when not imprisoning them for decades. That was the plan for Dhoruba as well. Yet, despite his nearly two decades in prison, he defied the state's plans. And, because he worked with Assata, he does not romanticize her or other women in the movement, although he acknowledges their work and, as is the case with Dhoruba, he criticizes everyone and everything. The reader can study his analyses, contributions, pointed observations of contradictions in terms of their relevance in our struggles of liberation.

In my book, *New Bones Abolition*, I discuss the surface of politics as the epicenter in which people organize for ethics, virtue, and civil rights seeking to stabilize the normative structure which originated through genocide, colonialism, enslavement, and imperialism.[3] I contrast the epicenter with the hypocenter, the "ground zero" of struggle against repression. Such struggles can be pacifist, as embodied in the revolutionary sacrifice of Martin Luther King, Jr., his condemnation of imperialism, capitalism, and his work for the poor people's campaign; or focused on self-defense, as advocated by el Hajj Malik el Shabazz/Malcolm X and who presciently observed in his 1963 "Message to the Grassroots: House Negro/Field Negro," what Dhoruba critiques in this book: betrayals by Black compradors. Decades ago, those who went into the underground—those committed to the "field negroes"—faced the most ruthless violence from the state and its police forces.

What Dhoruba Bin Wahad teaches in this book is what he collectively learned while engaged in liberation struggles with his comrades—those brother/sisters/two-spirit people moving towards revolutionary struggle, above ground, underground, within prisons and/or as spiritual markers, as ancestors who transitioned to the other side, but bequeathed an inheritance and legacy for freedom seekers. The rebel departure from the superficiality of surface politics led to the hypocenter, the ground zero of resistance against predatory violence. We need a bungie cord to link those who fear struggle or seek fortune to the revolutionaries who organize in the material world, pacifist and nonpacifist organizing against white nationalism, colonialism, imperialism, environmental devastation, and poverty. It would be great if we were all revolutionaries committed to the same program or platform to defeat colonialism and imperialism, LGBTQIA+ denigration, and premature death; it would be wonderful if we had a concerted campaign to stop genocide, feminicide, and ecocide. We are struggling. This is why it is important to study, and this is the importance of *Revolution in These Times*. At the epicenter, the surface of politics, governments, celebrities, elites and nonprofits with millions of dollars dominate and define, "influence," and steer political "radicalism." At the hypocenter, ground zero of revolutionary struggle, where Dhoruba ventured, those who engage in the material struggle sharpened their

3 Joy James, *New Bones Abolition: Captive Maternal Agency and the (After)life of Erica Garner* (Brooklyn and Philadelphia: Common Notions, 2023).

intellectualism and grappled with what constitutes ethics and commitments in a war zone.[4]

Dhoruba learned how to demystify oxymorons, as did his chief interlocutor in this text: Kalonji Changa, founder of both Black Power Media (BPM) and the FTP Movement, which celebrated its twentieth anniversary in June 2024. Changa and Bin Wahad have worked together for two decades to confront fascism, militarized policing, and varied forms of predation, including occupations, ethnic cleansing, and genocide.[5]

RESISTANCE IN OUR TIMES

I first met Dhoruba Bin Wahad in 1990, through BPP/BLA veteran Kim Holder, when he spoke at the University of Massachusetts-Amherst soon after his release from wrongful incarceration. I hosted him in my home. I would later rarely encounter him given his international organizing, but I recall the December 12th meetings in Harlem, and more recently, in addition to his texts, his interviews on Black Power Media and elsewhere.

When I suggested in 2022 that Black Power Media transcribe their interviews with Dhoruba and create a book that could bring attention to his knowledge and support the BLA veteran, they responded positively. Dhoruba offers facts, narratives, and analyses—intellectual, political, spiritual and physical—about war resistance and self-protections and what liberation might look like in our time and in our future. Elite and performative narratives will attempt to co-op his words and analyses. For now, we can read and study Dhoruba and reflect on spiritual warriors who remain on this side, flawed as human but—inshallah—blessed with courage and commitment for those seeking transformation.

—Joy James

---

4 *Still Black, Still Strong: Dhoruba Bin Wahad, Assata Shakur and Mumia Abu-Jamal*, ed. Jim Fletcher, Tanaquil Jones, and Sylvère Lotringer (New York: Semiotext(e), 1993) is another valuable text in which Dhoruba Bin Wahad's analyses and experiential knowledge are platformed.

5 See the 1951 *We Charge Genocide* document by the Black-led CPUSA Civil Rights Congress.

GLOSSARY

Black Liberation Army (BLA) was an underground, Black nationalist militant organization that operated in the United States from 1970 to 1981. The Black Liberation Army was not a centralized, organized group with a common leadership and chain of command. Instead, various organizations and collectives were working together and simultaneously independent of each other.

Black Panther Party (BPP), originally called the Black Panther Party for Self-Defense, was founded on October 15, 1966, by Huey P. Newton and Bobby Seale in Oakland, CA. Its ideology was heavily inspired by Malcolm X, Frantz Fanon, and other international freedom fighters. In September 1968, FBI Director J. Edgar Hoover described the Black Panthers as "the greatest threat to the internal security of the country." By 1969, the Black Panthers and their allies had become primary targets for assassinations and arrests as part of the FBI's counterinsurgency program "COINTELPRO."

Che-Lumumba Club, known as the Black cell of the Communist Party of the USA (CPUSA), originated from Black Communists in Los Angeles who fought within the CPUSA for a club that would be entirely Black and whose primary responsibility would be to carry Marxist-Leninist ideas to the Black Liberation struggle in LA and to provide leadership for the larger Party as far as the Black movement was concerned. The Che-Lumumba Club was named after Che Guevera and Patrice Lumumba.

CHESROB, the national anti-urban guerilla investigations collectively labeled under Joanne Chesimard's (Assata Shakur) name. CHESROB was aimed directly at destroying BLA soldiers and their clandestine infrastructure. By early 1972, the media labeled Chesimard the "soul" of the Black Liberation Army. Chesimard was named a suspect in virtually every New York City bank robbery where a woman was thought to have participated. Although "CHESROB" was designated as an FBI bank robbery investigation, it was really another coordinated

NYPD-FBI effort to capture or kill underground BPP members and BLA members.

COINTELPRO is an acronym for the FBI's Counterintelligence Program, a series of covert and illegal projects conducted between 1956 and 1971 by the United States Federal Bureau of Investigation (FBI) aimed at surveilling, infiltrating, discrediting, and disrupting political organizations that the FBI perceived as subversive.

COINTELPRO Task Force, or the National Taskforce for COINTELPRO Litigation and Research, led the struggle to expose COINTELPRO attacks on the Black Liberation struggle. By educating and organizing, and by coordinating lawsuits filed by Assata Shakur, the Republic of New Afrika 11, and others, the Task Force worked to expose the depths of government attacks and to free some of its major targets.

Communist Party USA emerged in 1919 as the left wing of the Socialist Party in the United States that split into the Communist Labor Party and the Communist Party of the United States. These two groups later merged into the Communist Party of the United States (CPUS) in 1921.

Congressional Black Caucus (CBC) was founded in 1971 and is made up of Black members of the United States Congress.

FTP Movement, established in June 2004, was formed in response to the United States government's disregard for the poor and oppressive conditions that support poverty. The FTP Movement's primary focus is to serve as an activator of the community. FTP Movement organizes survival and preparedness programs, fights against police terrorism, and advocates for political prisoners amongst a plethora of other issues.

Georgia International Law Enforcement Exchange (GILEE) has been in partnership with the University (headquartered inside the Andrew Young School of Policy Studies on the Georgia State University campus), Atlanta Police Department (as well as various other police agencies), public and corporate sectors, and civic groups since its inception thirty years ago. The privately controlled police exchange program provides local law enforcement with special training by Israeli Police Forces on the GSU campus which is conveniently located in the heart of downtown Atlanta.

Health Revolutionary Unity Movement (HRUM) began in October 1969 at New York City's Gouverneur Hospital as an organization of the hospital workers in opposition to the established hospital unions. In December of that year, HRUM decided to affiliate with the Young Lords Party and its work spread to half a dozen other city hospitals.

National Coalition to Combat Fascism grew out of the National Coalition to Combat Police Terrorism (NCCPT) which was established in 2015 by veteran Dhoruba Bin Wahad, former US Congresswoman Cynthia McKinney, and Kalonji Jama Changa. National Coalition to Combat Fascism is the lead coalition spearheading the United Front Against Fascism.

Operation Newkill, and the FBI acronym NEWKILL which stands for "New Killing of Police Officers," was concocted in 1971 by the Nixon White House to repress a "Black urban guerilla underground" in the wake of the urban rebellions (riots) that rocked America during the Vietnam war years. "Newkill" was a joint FBI-NYPD effort that became a model for later incarnations such as the "Joint Terrorism Taskforce."

Organization of African American Unity (OAAU) was a Pan-Africanist organization founded by Malcolm X in 1964. The OAAU was modeled after the Organization of African Unity, which Malcolm was introduced to during his visit to Africa.

Panther 21 consists of members of the Black Panther Party in New York City who, in April 1969, were charged with conspiracy to kill several police officers and to destroy a number of buildings. After two years in the courts, all of the defendants were acquitted.

Puerto Rican Nationalist Movement (PNPR) is a Puerto Rican political party founded on September 17, 1922, in San Juan, Puerto Rico. The PNPR's primary goal is to work for Puerto Rico's independence. In 1930, Pedro Albizu Campos was elected president of the PNPR and brought a radical change to the organization and its tactics.

Rainbow Coalition was a multicultural, working-class alliance of freedom fighters founded on the one-year anniversary of the assassination of Martin Luther King Jr., by Fred Hampton, Deputy Chairman of the Illinois chapter of the Black Panther Party. The Rainbow Coalition included the Black Panther Party, the Young Patriots, the Young Lords, Brown Berets, Students for a Democratic Society (SDS), the American

Indian Movement, and the Red Guard Party. The Rainbow Coalition was later hijacked by Jesse Jackson.

Republic of New Afrika (RNA) is a Black nationalist organization in the United States. The idea of the RNA arose following the events of the 1967 Detroit rebellion. It was the first separate nation declared by African Americans in the United States. On March 31, 1968, the Provisional Government was founded by more than five hundred New African leaders in Detroit, Michigan.

Revolutionary Action Movement was founded in 1963 by young activists led by Max Stanford (Muhammad Ahmad). RAM was a semi-clandestine organization and articulated a revolutionary program for Black Americans that fused Black Nationalism with Marxism-Leninism. Its goal was to develop revolutionary cadre in the Northern US and connect with more militant students in the US South. RAM supported the movement by SNCC and others for armed self-defense for Southern Blacks terrorized by the Ku Klux Klan as well as provided security for Malcolm X after his break from the Nation of Islam. RAM became one of the first casualties of the FBI's Counter-Intelligence Program (COINTELPRO). Max Stanford and other RAM leaders were charged with plotting to assassinate mainstream political leaders Roy Wilkins and Whitney Young. At this point, Stanford dissolved the formal structure of the organization.

Students for a Democratic Society (SDS), established in 1962, drew inspiration from the US civil rights movement. Its aim was to tackle poverty and the sense of helplessness, alienation, and indifference within African American and working-class communities. Initially focused on community organizing, the group soon emerged as a prominent figure in the antiwar movement when President Johnson intensified the war in Vietnam in 1965.

United Front Against Fascism is a moral alliance of groups against their common enemies. This coalition includes people from different backgrounds and political ideologies who share common goals, with a core value of resisting fascist ideologies and reducing corporate dominance in politics. By uniting, they can amplify their voices and work towards practical solutions.

Weather Underground Organization (WUO) was a clandestine, militant antiracist group formed in 1969 by members of Students for a Democratic Society (SDS). It aimed to overthrow US imperialism, aligning itself with the antiwar movement and supporting Third World liberation struggles. The WUO carried out bombings and other direct actions from the late 1960s to the mid-1970s and published various materials. The organization disbanded in 1976.

Young Lords Organization (YLO) was established in 1968 by José "Cha-Cha" Jiménez in Lincoln Park, Chicago. Modeled after the Black Panther Party (BPP), the YLO evolved from a street gang into a national community-based organization advocating for Puerto Rican, Latino, and colonized access to healthcare, education, housing, and employment.

Young Patriots Organization (YPO), founded in 1968 by Uptown Chicago's white Southerners and their allies, organized in opposition to the stereotypes that they were ignorant "hillbillies" and hopeless racists. Uptown had some of the worst poverty in the city and living conditions were grim with hunger and poor health for many. The Young Patriots grew out of the work of the Uptown JOIN organization, a unique collaboration between white migrants from Appalachia and young radicals from the Students for a Democratic Society (SDS). First organized in 1964, JOIN organized community meetings, marches, rent strikes, pickets, and civil disobedience to protest the poverty-producing policies of the Mayor Richard J. Daley democratic machine and its corporate sponsors.

Youth Against War and Fascism (YAWF) is the youth organization associated with the Workers World Party. Founded in 1962, YAWF carried its orange banners in the many confrontational actions of the 1960s and 1970s opposing the war in Vietnam, in solidarity with the Black Liberation Movement in the United States, and in solidarity with all the movements around the world fighting for self-determination and liberation from imperialism.

LIST OF FIGURES

Mumia Abu-Jamal, a veteran Black Panther and journalist who was convicted in 1982 for the murder of Philadelphia police officer Daniel Faulkner, a case surrounded by controversy and allegations of racial bias and judicial misconduct. Over the years, he has become a symbol in the fight for prison reform and racial justice, advocating for his innocence from death row through his writings and media appearances. His case has attracted international attention, raising important questions about the fairness of the legal system and the treatment of political prisoners.

Sundiata Acoli, a veteran Black Panther and Black Liberation Army member. On May 2, 1973, Sundiata, Assata Shakur, and Zayd Malik Shakur were ambushed by state troopers on the New Jersey Turnpike. During the incident, Zayd was murdered and Assata was shot and seriously wounded. Trooper Werner Foerster was killed by the bullets from a state trooper's gun. Sundiata Acoli was convicted of Foerster's murder and sentenced to life. After forty-nine years in prison, Acoli was finally granted parole in May 2022 at the age of eighty-five.

Alajo Adegbalola served as Minister of Defense (1970) and first Vice President (1971–1972) of the Provisional Government of the Republic of New Afrika (PGRNA). The fearless General Alajo introduced the concept of the People's Army within the RNA, ensuring that all its citizens had military training. Alajo was the father of Fulani Sunni-Ali.

Imam Jamil Al-Amin, formerly known as H. Rap Brown, is a prominent figure in the human rights movement and has had a significant impact on social justice and activism globally. Al-Amin became known for his fiery speeches and leadership as a chairman of the Student Nonviolent Coordinating Committee (SNCC) during the tumultuous 1960s. Over time, he converted to Islam and adopted the name Jamil Al-Amin. In 2000, Al-Amin was falsely accused and convicted of murdering a deputy sheriff in Georgia. He is currently serving a life sentence.

Kuwasi Balagoon, a veteran member of the Black Panther Party and defendant in the Panther 21 case. Balagoon went underground with the Black Liberation Army (BLA), but he was captured and convicted of various crimes against the state. He spent much of the 1970s in prison, escaping twice. After each escape, he went underground and resumed BLA activity. Balagoon was captured for the last time in December 1981, charged with participating in an armored truck expropriation in West Nyack, New York, an action in which two police officers and a money courier were killed. Convicted and sentenced to life imprisonment, he died of an AIDS-related illness on December 13, 1986.

Herman Bell, a veteran member of the Black Panther Party who was involved in the Black Liberation Movement during the late 1960s and early 1970s. He was convicted in 1971 for the killing of two police officers in San Francisco and was sentenced to life in prison. In 2018, he was granted parole after serving nearly forty-seven years in prison.

Veronza Bowers, Jr., veteran Black Panther sentenced to life in prison in 1973 for the murder of a US park ranger, based on testimony from government informants. He was released in May 2024, at age seventy-eight, after serving over fifty years in prison.

Angela Yvonne Davis, a prominent political activist in the 1960s and 1970s, gained national attention in 1969 after being dismissed from her UCLA teaching role for her Communist Party affiliation. She faced serious charges in 1970 that led to an international campaign for her release, and was ultimately acquitted in 1972.

Flo Kennedy, a groundbreaking lawyer and advocate for civil and women's rights, was known for founding the Media Workshop to combat advertising racism, representing significant figures like H. Rap Brown and the Black Panthers, and establishing the Feminist Party, which nominated Congresswoman Shirley Chisholm for president in 1972.

Larry Mack, a veteran Black Panther/BLA member who was a codefendant in the New York Panther 21 case.

Ruchell Cinque Magee was a freedom fighter who was involved in the August 7, 1970, Marin County Courthouse rebellion. In 2023, at eighty-three years old, US political prisoner "Cinque" Magee was released from prison after sixty-seven years. Magee died three months later.

Jalil Muntaqim, a former Black Panther and BLA member, spent over forty-nine years in prison after being convicted of first-degree murder in 1975 for the deaths of two NYPD officers, but he was finally released on October 7, 2020, after being eligible for parole since 1993.

Twymon Myers, a Black Liberation Army member recruited by Thomas "Blood" McCreary at twenty, was accused of killing two police officers in New York in 1972 and subsequently placed on the FBI's Ten Most Wanted Fugitives list before being killed in a gun battle with the NYPD and the FBI in the Bronx.

Sekou Odinga, a prominent figure in Malcolm X's Organization of Afro-American Unity, the Black Panther Party, and the Black Liberation Army, was convicted in 1984 for aiding Assata Shakur's escape. Odinga served thirty-three years in prison and was released in 2014. He made his transition in January 2024.

Geronimo Ji-Jagga Pratt, a veteran Black Panther Party member, wrongfully convicted of murder in 1972, spent nearly twenty-seven years in prison before his conviction was overturned in 1997 due to prosecutorial misconduct, bringing attention to racial injustice and systemic failures in the criminal justice system, which he continued to address until his death on June 2, 2011.

Queen Mother Audley Moore, an influential African American civil and human rights leader and Black nationalist, collaborated with prominent figures like Marcus Garvey and Rosa Parks, played a pivotal role in the American Civil Rights Movement, cofounded the Republic of New Afrika, and is celebrated as the "Mother" of the modern Reparations Movement.

Gloria Richardson was a prominent civil rights leader who earned a sociology degree from Howard University in 1942 and significantly contributed to the Cambridge Movement of the 1960s while advocating for civil and economic rights in her community.

Kamau Sadiki joined the Black Panther Party at age sixteen in Queens, NYC, and in 2002, he turned down a $1 million FBI bounty to aid in the capture of Assata Shakur—his daughter's mother—resulting in his arrest on false charges and a life sentence.

Afeni Shakur was a pivotal figure in the Black Liberation Movement, known for her activism with the Black Panther Party, and her notable defense in the Panther 21 trial. She was the mother of hip-hop legend Tupac Shakur.

Assata Shakur the Black Panther/BLA veteran Assata Olugbala Shakur, was stopped (along with Zayd Shakur and Sundiata Acoli) by New Jersey State Police, shot twice, and subsequently charged with murdering an officer. After enduring six and a half years in harsh prison conditions, she was liberated from a maximum-security facility in 1979 and sought refuge in Cuba. Shakur currently has a $2 million bounty for her apprehension.

Mutulu Shakur joined the New Afrikan Independence Movement (NAIM) at sixteen and was active in the Revolutionary Action Movement (RAM). Dr. Shakur was a founding citizen of the Republic of New Afrika. Dr. Shakur got involved in helping political education initiatives in New York City, being able to contribute to the Black Panther Party even while not being a formal member of the party. He also was an active leader in the Black Liberation Army (BLA).

El Hajj Sallahudin Shakur was an associate of El Hajj Malik Shabazz (Malcolm X), he was a member of the Muslim Mosque Incorporated and also a member of the Organization of Afro-American Unity. He is the progenitor of the Shakur family tree.

Russell "Maroon" Shoatz, inspired by Malcolm X, became a lifelong crusader for justice, a soldier in the most militant units of the Black Liberation Army. Shoatz was convicted to life in prison following a coordinated attack on a park police station that left one guard dead. He escaped state prisons twice, making him a living legend, and endowed him with the moniker "Maroon," once used to honor runaway slaves from plantations. He survived twenty-two years in solitary confinement, prompting an international campaign for his freedom.

Fulani Sunni Ali joined the Black Panther Party for Self-Defense at nineteen and became a founding member of the Republic of New Africa, dedicated her life to various roles—including priest, midwife, journalist, and human rights activist—while passionately advocating for Black liberation. At the time of her transition, Fulani was the Commanding General of the Black Legion and the International Commanding General of the Belizian post of the Black Legion.

Michael "Cetewayo" Tabor joined the Black Panther Party in 1969 and took the name Cetewayo, after the nineteenth-century Zulu Warrior King. According to former members, Tabor was one of the more well known of the spokespersons for the Panther Party. Tabor was one of the twenty-one members of the New York Chapter of the Panthers who were indicted in April 1969. In February 1971, while out on bail, Tabor flew to Algiers, Algeria in fear of his life due to the illegal FBI COINTELPRO-induced internal conflicts that were developing within the Black Panther Party. Several months later, the twenty-one defendants were acquitted of all charges.

Albert Nuh Washington, or "Nuh" (the Arabic form of Noah), was an active member of the Black Panther Party who later collaborated with the Black Liberation Army. He was unjustly convicted of murder alongside Jalil Muntaqim and Herman Bell after being shot and captured in the 1970s, spending over twenty-eight years in prisons in California and New York where he faced repeated punishment for his political beliefs.

Robert Williams was a militant civil rights leader from Monroe, North Carolina, who championed armed self-defense and influenced the Black Power Movement of the late 1960s. As president of his local NAACP branch, Williams aimed to cultivate a membership that reflected his vision of a working-class, militant, and armed community, distinctly different from the moderate, middle-class membership of the national group. Williams' efforts inspired groups like the Student National Coordinating Committee, the Revolutionary Action Movement, and the Black Panther Party.

1

LESSONS FROM THE BLACK LIBERATION TRADITION

Black leadership, state repression, and self-defense

> *"The gun was never seen as a means. The gun, basically, was looked upon as an instrument to galvanize, revolutionize, and educate Black people."*

KALONJI: We are here rumbling in this wild jungle, across multiple continents, trying to survive imperialism, you know what it looks like out here. Dr. Mutulu Shakur made his transition.[1] Give us some insights and feedback on who Dr. Mutulu Shakur was and what he meant to the movement and what his transition means.

DHORUBA: Well, Dr. Mutulu—may Allah be pleased with him, may he rest in power—has been in our struggle for a long time. He was one of the core cadres in the Republic of New Afrika for decades. He participated in most of the RNA's activities during the '60s. He was very close with many of our comrades in the Black Panther Party before they were in the Party, like Sekou Odinga, Bilal Sunni Ali, Abdul Majid, and many of the other comrades.

Mutulu got involved with us and the Young Lords in New York around 1969, when we opened up Lincoln Detox Center in the South Bronx. It was opened by the Black Panthers, the Young Lords, the RNA, and some members of the radical white left. With the Health Revolutionary Unity Movement, we took over Lincoln Hospital, a drug rehabilitation center, and one of the first

1 Dr. Mutulu Shakur, New Afrikan revolutionary, acupuncturist, and visionary theorist, passed on July 7, 2023. He was active in Black Liberation Army (BLA) leadership and contributed to the activities of the Black Panther Party chapter in New York City.

methadone clinics in New York at that time.[2] Methadone was heralded as the drug that would stop the white plague, stop the plague in its tracks. In fact, it was a substitute for heroin.

In New York, drug addicts were sentenced to rehabilitation, drug treatment, methadone maintenance. They became state dope fiends. They became state drug addicts. We had a problem with that, because we felt that drug addiction was a mental health issue. We understood that exploitation, white supremacy, racism, and the dynamics of the domestic colonization of African people had created mental health issues amongst African people, amongst poor people. These health issues led to high rates of drug addiction, not to mention the fact that the Black community was targeted for the distribution of heroin by the CIA, the State Department, and by organized crime.

Drug addiction—mainly heroin addiction at that time—was at its height in 1969. When the methadone clinic, this new building, came up in Lincoln Hospital in the Southeast Bronx, we occupied the premises. We barricaded our comrades in and we occupied the premises. We started doing political education classes with the drug addicts who were in the program there. It lasted for several years. Dr. Mutulu Shakur came on board and added his acupuncture skills.

When Lincoln Detox Center faded—I believe it might have been 1972—Dr. Shakur took his skills and established later on in that decade the COINTELPRO Task Force, which he supervised and managed along with Sister Afeni Shakur.[3] Mutulu has always tried to be in the forefront of our struggle on a level that many other comrades weren't. I'm talking about the acupuncture skills, dealing with the health issues of our comrades, of oppressed people. He was trying to understand how we could create institutions in our community—free health programs, free breakfast programs, and these various other programs that we tried to implement—as

2 The Health Revolutionary Unity Movement (HRUM) began in October 1969 as an autonomous organization of Puerto Rican and Black hospital workers of Local 1199 of the Drug and Hospital Workers Union in New York's Governor Hospital. Affiliated with the Young Lords party, they helped occupy Lincoln Hospital on July 14, 1970.

3 The COINTELPRO Task Force on Research and Litigation was focused on fighting state repression.

examples to our people of what could be done if we mobilized our own resources and relied upon ourselves to cure our illnesses and protect ourselves from the ravages of white supremacy. Dr. Mutulu Shakur was a full-fledged citizen and a leader of the Republic of New Africa. He was also a writer. He wrote a number of very insightful articles.[4]

I was in the BPP, so our relationship was not an organizational one. But we shared a common pool of comrades, so to speak—Sekou Odinga, Larry Mack, Lumumba Shakur, and others. They all came out of South Jamaica and Brooklyn. That's where Dr. Mutulu Shakur grew up. He had an early relationship with the Organization of African American Unity and Malcolm X.

KALONJI: Since I got the news on Dr. Mutulu Shakur my chest has had this knot in it. It's a cross between pain over his loss and disgust with our movement. There are many folks in my era that came up under you all, and we know better. We were able to learn from OGs and elders. We were able to learn from folks like the Elombe Brath, Amiri Baraka, Baba Herman Fergusons to the Dr. Bens and the Dr. Clarks.

A lot of folks today are playing although we've watched you as a political prisoner, we watched Mutulu as a political prisoner. We had the posters of you all: Marilyn Buck, Mumia, and Russell Shoatz, and Ruchell Magee who was locked up sixty-plus years. How do we balance this thing without going over the edge?

DHORUBA: It's very painful to have to talk about Mutulu in the past tense. One of the reasons why, is because many of our brothers and sisters who were incarcerated, came out of prison and transitioned shortly thereafter. The prison authorities didn't want to accept the responsibility and the costs for them dying in their prison when, in fact, they contributed to it. They did everything they could to bring about the demise of our comrade. I just want to say that it's because of the weakness of the political prisoner issue in the United States, of the movement to free our political prisoners, that Dr. Mutulu Shakur only was freed as a matter of so-called

4 See the special issue of *Soul* (Vol. 23, no 1–2, January–June 2022), guest edited by Akinyele Umoja and Susan Rosenberg on Dr. Mutulu Shakur's life and legacy. Addition writings can be found at Freedom Archives and Prison Radio.

mercy by the state, rather than being freed by the power of our movement. This is very sad. It would be disingenuous if I were to say that the efforts to free our political prisoners is what got Dr. Mutulu Shakur out of jail. It wasn't. We still have Imam Jamil Al-Amin in prison who is suffering from severe illnesses. We have our brother Kamau Sadiki and Mumia Abu Jamal, who is undergoing a severe medical crisis.

These brothers and sisters have been in prison for decades and are now elderly and in infirm health because we have not challenged the so-called Black political class, our so-called elected leaders, many of whom are prosecutors in our community, some of whom are working with the state as prosecutors. They were appointed by Black mayors. We have Black mayors, Black prosecutors, Black judges. Yet, we have not held them accountable for their failure to deal with our community and change the racist, reactionary class system of law enforcement.

Many of these individuals claim that they go into these jobs to change the atmosphere, to bring about change. We know that's all bullshit. They wind up going in and becoming part of the problem. They wind up going and covering up for the institutions and running interference for those institutions.

It's clear that one individual in an institution like the NYPD or the New York court system is not going to change that system from within. He or she is not going to do that. Then we have the other side of that, when some of these brothers or sisters get their law degrees and they go into these professions in law enforcement and the courts and the judiciary as parole officers or whatever, they never use that position to inform the Black community about what is going on inside those institutions that are detrimental to the well-being of our communities.

They will not give us the heads-up, for instance, on the undercurrent of policies that are designed to neutralize our political well-being, to neutralize us as a community, because all politics is local, that's very important. We've always maintained that the police—especially the armed agents of the state, these individuals who consider themselves law enforcement officers, these idiots in blue costumes, running around our community, brutalizing us, murdering us, beating us, harassing our families—are part and parcel of institution that is designed to maintain control of our communities. Our elected officials, many of who kowtow and bow down to the police unions and law enforcement in order to get elected and to get endorsements from these unions, wind up catering to these racist institutions more than they react and respond to the needs of their own constituents and communities.

When we talked about public safety and community control of public safety, it were brothers like Mutulu Shakur and Sekou Odinga, and other brothers and sisters who were in the Party, who were in RNA, who laid down the radical tradition, the radical history, the radical approach to how we should do this.

KALONJI: It would seem like we would know better. It's like we're moving backwards right now. Everything is personality-driven. Why do you think we're stuck in this particular conundrum? How do we escape this?

DHORUBA: Because we haven't had real movements—now, when I say "real," I don't mean that the so-called movements that are present today somehow don't exist. It's just that their politics is not based on our radical tradition and history, nor informed by those battles and struggles that we already won and are now confronted with again, in camouflage and in a different persona. We don't have organizations that address all of these facets of our community and come together with a strategic program and a strategic plan to empower our community and take control of the institutions.

Our comrades, many of them who have been in the trenches fighting for political prisoners for years, who have been visiting the political prisoners, who have been putting on forums for the political prisoners, need to understand that we are not part of the political discussion in America. The reason for this is because the political elite in America chooses to ignore our radical history and tradition and to create a false, stealth history of those struggles that makes them look good, that makes them look progressive. It makes them powerful.

I'm saying, if we want the recognition of our political prisoners, we have to hold those elected officials who come into our communities and our constituencies accountable. They should not be able to show their face in our community unless they're doing something concrete for our political prisoners, or in the community. I think that it's time that we get some drop squads out here. I'm advocating that we protest the lack of political leadership, that we protest the relevant Black faces in high places.

Only when we begin to really become part of this discussion, this debate, this national debate, on which way the Black community has to go to empower itself, can we put the issue of political prisoners to the forefront. No movement is a genuine movement for freedom and liberation if it doesn't put the issue of their political freedom fighters who are in prison and captured, first. Nelson Mandela didn't get out of prison after they dismantled the apartheid. He got out of prison before they did, because it was a condition that he get out, you see. We have to do that.

Our comrades are dying in prison, our comrades are being forgotten. Then we're going to have these pork-chop preachers and everyone talking about saving souls and how we have to empower ourselves, but they never once mention our political prisoners. They never mention once Imam Jamil al-Amin. They never once mention Mumia Abu-Jamal.

When we don't have mass movements, when we don't have a united front and broad-based coalitions that transcend class—in other words, coalitions between working-class Africans in the United States and the diaspora, and African professionals in the diaspora, as well as unemployed lumpenproletariat on the streets, we are not going to achieve any type of self-determination, any type of control over our community. We have not been able to fully avail ourselves of the panoply of resistance, of instruments and tools of resistance, precisely because we don't have a revolutionary or even abolitionist movement or a united front with leadership with principled collectives.

KALONJI: What are the lessons we need to learn today from the leadership structure of the BPP? How do we account for the backlash that militant leaders faced?

DHORUBA: When Chairman Fred Hampton was assassinated in Chicago on December 4, 1969, the Black Panther Party was going through the development of a system of democratic centralism. In this process, the leadership of the Party at that time—which was predominantly in California—realized that it had to become more representative of its chapters and its branches across the country and have their leadership participate in the National Party. Organizing it, leading the BPP nationally.

Fred Hampton was one of those brothers, one of those comrades who was earmarked to become a member of the Central Committee of the Party. I believe that the enemy knew that. I believe that they knew how charismatic and how politically astute Fred was for his age. They felt that they had to nip that in the bud. I mean, there were other factors involved, but that's what was happening in '69 in the US regarding the BPP. We were about to democratize the central committee, with leaders from different communities and different chapters from around the country who would be reposted to California. Fred was one of those that was chosen.

Fred Hampton's assassination was an FBI game plan. It was part of a broader FBI strategy to intimidate and to discourage the development of revolutionary consciousness amongst African youth. In fact, they put out a memo to that effect right before Fred was assassinated. This infamous memorandum was a counterintelligence eerie tale. It said that the FBI had to do everything in its power to prove to Black youth that if they succumb to revolutionary teachings, they would be dead revolutionaries.

We know from the experience of the BLA and the underground that the police has always gone to organized crime in order to try to defeat us. But because we grew up with a lot of these gangsters, they would tell us this. They would tell us that the police from Boston, the Major Case Squad, pulled them over, took them into the police station, or pulled them over and told them, "Look, if you don't give us these cop killers, you ain't going to handle drugs out here. We're going to bust every worker that you got, and you're going to jail, too. We want to know who these people are." The first place they went were to the criminals. The first place they went were to the illegitimate capitalists and said, "You ain't going to do business if we don't get these cop killers." That's exactly what the illegitimate capitalists did. They did everything they could to inform on us, but because there's an inherent hatred of the police, even by the criminal elements, they felt awkward snitching. Snitching was like amoral. They would tell us, "Hey man, these people, they hot out here, man. They got all my workers, they just bust in. They want information. I know you since we was in junior high school, bro. I ain't going, but I don't have control over everybody in the street. Now, they be snitching."

When somebody like Jamil Al-Amin moves into Atlanta and takes over the whole area and makes the streets safe for ordinary people, they put him in jail. He's been in for what? Imam Jamil has been in jail twenty-something years now? This is H. Rap Brown. This is where you get the name for your music from. Rap Brown. The reason why he got that because he could talk, and he could break stuff down. Every time he broke stuff down, people burn shit down.

They passed a whole act, a congressional act. Interstate travel to incite riots, the Rap Brown Law, go look it up. It's named after a Black man who's in jail right now. The average person on the street right now, who's getting pulled over by the police, was getting harassed by the police, doesn't even know Rap Brown exists. Doesn't even know he's still alive.

This was a clear strategy by the FBI and the US government to discourage the development of revolutionary leadership amongst Black youth. This was very important. That game plan worked. The establishment sent a clear message that it would be better if the average youth would become a sports star or entertainment figure—a dancer or a singer—that white Americans could care for and love and elevate, than to be a revolutionary who was despised by the system and despised by those who controlled the system.

This reminds me of Jay-Z, who was born on the same day Hampton was assassinated. Jay-Z has become one of the most prominent and wealthiest young men to emerge from the hip hop scene and from rap music. He's done that. He's a very talented young man. His wife, Beyoncé Knowles, is a very talented sister. They have transformed and changed a lot of the entertainment industry regarding Black music and hip hop. I think it's worth noting that pimping Black culture has long been an old-school pimp game. Pimping Black culture and lifestyle to white society and the broader culture in general has always been part and parcel of the institutional game plan in America—at least since the 1950s, with the advent of Malcolm X. Malcolm X was the most significant figure that inspired or motivated the system to understand that anyone who would become a revolutionary, who would become a Black nationalist or a Pan-Africanist, had to be eliminated, had to be criminalized and marginalized. This is still going on today.

If we notice, in terms of the electoral system, the recent elections, the bootlickers and the soft-shoe artists from the Democratic Party came out in unison to say that the reason why they didn't fare so well in Congress was because of convenient slogans, slogans that talked about defunding police and Black power turned off voters. This turned off a whole section of the community that wasn't with them. It's very important that we understand that this was all part of the game plan, and that the enemy—the system of white supremacy—has institutional memory and it remembers these things. Whereas our activists, our young people, were cut off from their radical tradition and their radical memory.

When we're talking about Fred Hampton today, we're basically going over what we know they planned all the time. What most African and young people today don't even realize is what they are playing into. We could see that when we have ignorant fools like Lil Wayne and 50 Cent, these different artists who came out for Trump, to talk about dealing with the right wing. As if it's the same as the left, as if there's no difference, and as if money itself is the access to liberation.

KALONJI: When folks talk about the assassination of Chairman Fred, they talk about the Panthers that were vamped on in LA and the Panther 21 as separate events. They thought that you all were, as in the case of Chairman Fred, just charismatic speakers and nicely organized and that it wasn't a concerted effort. It has been over fifty years since the Panther 21 situation went down in April 1969. Can you talk to us a little bit about what the Panther 21 case was about?

DHORUBA: Basically, the Panther 21 was an indictment mainly against the Harlem branch in the security section of the Black Panther Party in New York City. It was initiated by the NYPD and their Bureau of Special Services, BOSS, which was the intelligence agency of the NYPD. They also participated in the assassination of Malcolm X, in steadying up the Harlem Pride, and in the Statue of Liberty case.[5] BOSS was a very active undercover police operation and intelligence agency. It was actively involved in repression and

10 For more on the Bureau of Special Services, BOSS, and its response to the antiwar and Black Power movements of the 1960s, see Frank Donner, *Protectors of Privilege: Red Squads and Police Repression in Urban America* (Berkeley, CA: University of California, 1992).

suppression. Later, as we see from the counterintelligence records and the accounts of the joint terrorist task force, which were put together in 1971, it was also a participant in a number of assassinations and murders of Black activists in New York City.

The Panther 21 case was basically an operation carried out against the Black Panther Party by the NYPD and its intelligence apparatus. Now, the FBI and their Counterintelligence Program were not intimately involved in the framing of the Panther 21, but they were involved in putting the Panther 21 in the spotlights.

People need to understand that the Panther 21 were not indicted because we were the ranking, or that we were the leadership in New York. That's not true. Much of the leadership in New York were not among the Panther 21. It was mainly the security section in New York, which was involved in securing the offices and the Black Panther Party newspapers and operations that were targeted. This was in conjunction with an overall government plan to disrupt the Black Panther Party's leadership and to prevent the party's central committee from becoming democratized at that particular point in time. That's also what led to the assassination of Fred Hampton, the indictment of Bobby Seale in New Haven, and to the Chicago 7 Trial where he was bound and gagged as a consequence of him speaking at the Republican National Convention.

KALONJI: This case was at the time the longest case in New York history, correct?

DHORUBA: That's true.

KALONJI: The longest and most expensive case in New York history. Why would you say that was?

DHORUBA: It was a conspiracy. It involved weaving a web of fallacies and perceptions so that the jury could believe that Black Panthers were going to blow up flowers in the botanical garden, that we were going to plant bombs in Abercrombie and Fitch, and we were going to blow up the subway system that the working class in New York City used to get to work. They fabricated these charges based on the infiltration in the BPP by undercover agents and their knowledge of the training procedures and the training operations of the BPP security section. We need to understand that this type of case requires collusion between the judge, the district attorney, and various agencies of government in order to fabricate these charges.

Of course, we didn't cooperate. We would regularly disrupt the court and they would have to close down the proceedings. Then reconvene them and at one point, they closed down the proceedings until we wrote an apology. Instead, we wrote an analysis of white supremacy and the legal justice system and presented it to the court when it reconvened the session. That was right before I left and went underground.

KALONJI: There were 156 charges, correct? Right after this case, after these charges, you were framed again. Was that a week after the cases where acquitted?

DHORUBA: We were acquitted on May 13 and six days later, on May 19—Malcolm X's birthday—two New York City policemen guarding the home of Frank Hogan were shot and seriously wounded. Frank Hogan was the iconic district attorney in New York City who prosecuted the Panther 21. Right after that, on May 21, two other policemen were shot and killed in a Harlem project. It was these two cases that brought together the federal government and local law enforcement to create the Joint Anti-Terrorist Task Force and they launched an investigation they called Newkill.[6] It was a kind of intelligence program directly aimed at criminalizing and assassinating Black Panther activists as fugitives from US law enforcement. It was conceived in the offices of Richard Nixon, the president at that time. They convened a meeting and they came up with Operation Newkill, basically a counter-insurgency pro-criminal investigation. It was aimed at the emerging Black Liberation Army, the BLA, which came into existence in 1971, after the rift

6 See Friends of the New York Three, "Prisoners of War: The Case of the New York Three," *Roz Payne Sixties Archive*, https://rozsixties.unl.edu/items/show/451. Of the five men arrested as a result of Operation Newkill, three were active targets of FBI's COINTELPRO operations as members of the BPP and BLA: Jalil Muntaqim, Albert "Nuh" Washington, and Herman Bell. All three were arrested, convicted, and served long sentences in federal prisons. Jalil Muntaqim is currently on parole after being incarcerated for half a century at Attica Correctional Facility and Southport Correctional Facility. Albert "Nuh" Washington spent twenty-nine years of his life as a political prisoner before passing away from cancer. Herman Bell was granted parole and released from Shawangunk Prison in April 2018.

and split in the BPP became irreconcilable. There's a lot to unpack there. Some things can't be said because there is no statute of limitations.

Basically, it was six days after the Panther 21 were acquitted on May 13 that these officers were shot. A few days later, Operation Newkill was instituted, and they went after the Panther 21, the political prisoners of RNA, the SDS and the Weather Underground, and they went after the Puerto Rican Nationalist Movement. All of these operations were carried out by the Joint Anti-Terrorist Task Force of the federal government, the NYPD, the Chicago Police Department, and other agencies.

KALONJI: What was the role of COINTELPRO in these cases?

DHORUBA: Well, there's a lot to unpack. In relationship to Fred Hampton and the Chicago Black Panther Party, we do know that the agent, William O'Neal, was also on the payroll of the FBI. He provided the Chicago FBI Counterintelligence and Racial Matters desk of the Chicago Police Department with the layout of the Panther pad that led to the raid and the murder of Fred Hampton and Mark Clark.

Now, people on the surface would say that Fred Hampton and Mark Clark were killed because they were charismatic young Black leaders, that they had to be eliminated much like Malcolm and other Black leaders were killed and eliminated. But that is not the crux of it. The crux of it was that at that particular point in time, eight months before Fred was murdered, the Panther 21 were indicted. When the Panther 21 were indicted in New York, Bobby Seale came through the city on his way to New Haven to do a speaking engagement. He reviewed the situation in New York and came to the conclusion that they should close the New York chapter of the BPP because it was heavily infiltrated by the police. Of course, people like myself, Sekou Odinga, and others totally disagreed with that. We felt that Harlem was the capital, the cultural and political center of Black America, of Africans in the United States. For the BPP not to have a chapter in Harlem would be unthinkable. It would be ridiculous. It would show a severe weakness in the party. David, Bobby, and others decided to keep the chapter open and send organizers from other chapters to pull the party back together in the wake of the 21 arrests.

Bobby went on to New Haven to speak. While he was in New Haven, the federal government and COINTELPRO lured Bobby into the basement where an undercover agent and others had kidnapped Alex Rackley from New York and brought him to New Haven. According to court records and accounts, they were engaged in torturing Alex Rackley, and he supposedly confessed to knowing all the informers in New York. Bobby saw what was happening, of course, and he didn't want to have anything to do with it. He went back upstairs and told this agent to deal with it. An agent killed Alex Rackley. He involved other partners in this heinous crime. This agent went from chapter to chapter, causing this mayhem. Bobby was caught up in that, right after he had spoken at the Republican National Convention. It's in the same period of time.

Of course, we know about the police riot in Chicago during the Republican National Convention in 1969 and how an indictment was brought against the white radicals and Bobby Seale for instigating a so-called riot at the convention. This indictment was brought against Bobby after he was arrested for conspiracy to kill Alex Rackley in New Haven. All of this stems from the arrest of the 21 and from the fact that during this particular time, there was an internal struggle to undo the effects the Counterintelligence Program was having on the party with agent provocateurs, with saboteurs and everything.

When the Panther 21 were arrested, the ranks of the BPP were closed. Anybody that came to work in a Panther chapter were called community workers. They weren't called Black Panther members. They had to go through a period of community worker status before they would become full-time members.

The closing of the New York chapter and the attacks on the BPP forced many of us to urge the Central Committee to become more democratic, to become more representative of its chapters. The party had grown exponentially since Huey P. Newton was arrested, when it had over a dozen chapters around the country. In each chapter, the members that came together to form that chapter had been activists in those communities before they became Panthers. They were organizers like Fred Hampton. We could say they were charismatic. They had skill sets, too. There was a push to have these types of leaders on the local level become actual members of the central committee, to guide the party, and to command the party's direction.

The FBI knew about this. They knew what would happen if leaders like Fred Hampton, myself, Sekou Odinga, or other brothers in Denver, in Seattle, in other chapters, had become official members of the central committee and what that would mean for the BPP. That was why Fred Hampton was assassinated when he was. That was why the BPP were indicted and arrested on those spurious crazy charges when they were. That's why Bobby Seale was taken off the streets and imprisoned. It was for those reasons: to destroy the BPP's ability to lead the New Left and to lead the revolutionary movement in the United States, by having an effective and national democratic central leadership.

KALONJI: I'd like to return to the topic of building national democratic central leadership and the question of a third political party, but first I want to dig a bit deeper into COINTELPRO and how it connects to you.

DHORUBA: I was still field secretary of the BPP in Harlem and for the East Coast. I traveled around the East Coast a lot. A few times to Chicago, but that was basically my role before I got busted in the Panther 21 case before the conspiracy case came down. What happened was I filed a suit in 1975, when the story broke on COINTELPRO about the Media, Pennsylvania break-ins.[7]

I was in the box in Comstock when that news broke and my attorney Robert Bloom, he was one of the Panther 21 attorneys, a people's lawyer, came to visit me one time and I showed him the article. After he read that, I said, "Bob we know that I'm in here on trumped up charges. Why don't we file a suit, demanding the release of my COINTELPRO files? I'm sure they've got some on the Black Panther Party." He took that and he went to the Center for Constitutional Rights, which, at that time, had considered the BLA and the BPP criminals and thugs. They were reluctant to do the suit. But because Bob Bloom had prestige with them as

7 Activists referring to themselves as the Citizens' Commission to Investigate the FBI broke into the agency's office in Media, PA, in 1971, and recovered over one thousand classified documents exposing illegal FBI investigations and the agency's extensive COINTELPRO operations.

an attorney—a white, Jewish attorney—they humored him. They allowed him to use their facilities and their name to file a civil suit.[8]

The net result was that they moved to have this suit dismissed, the government, Southern District of New York. In order to dismiss the suit, they said that it was without merit, that the suit had no merit, that I was just a common criminal. That the only records they had on me were my criminal records, and that suit should be dismissed. The mistake that they made—and again this is historical—the mistake that they made was they brought this argument before Mary Johnson Lowe, one of the first Black female appointees to the federal court, I believe she was appointed by Lyndon Baines Johnson. She was on the legal team of Thurgood Marshall in their historical suit of *Brown v. Board of Education*. Mary Johnson Lowe was no joke. This sister, she considered all of the facts about the case, and she was on the verge of saying, "As all they got is his criminal record there's not much I can do based on the evidence."

At that time, Dennis Cunningham—who was once in the collective of the Panther 21 lawyers—and some other lawyers in Chicago, were processing Fred Hampton's suit against the FBI and the Chicago Police Department. They were in the discovery phase of that suit when they got documents from the FBI. It had the counterintelligence program on it, and, of course, by then everybody knew that it existed, but it also had my name on these documents. They sent us copies of these documents and we showed them to Mary Johnson Lowe, and Sister Lowe went off on the US Attorney. She said, "You stood up in front of me for weeks and just lied straight away. You said you had no documents, and you searched everything, and you don't have no documents with this man's name on it."

She was insulted, as a matter of fact, that she was a judge and that the US Attorney misrepresented this. She demanded that they turn over everything that they had in the FBI files, on the BPP, wherever it was, and whomever it belonged to, and especially mine. I spent the next year and a half at the Metropolitan Correctional Facility in Lower Manhattan, reading documents for a year and a half. I got 700,000 pages of FBI files.

---

8 See *Bin Wahad v. FBI*, et al., 75 Civ. 6203 [U.S. District Court for the Southern District of New York], January 29, 1993..

It was going through these files and we found out that the government had framed me, that they had manufactured the case against me because while they were manufacturing the case against me, while they were framing me, the FBI was there taking notes all the time because they were working together. But the FBI was left out of the state prosecution, and they just laid back.

KALONJI: Turning back to the question of effective and national democratic central leadership, what about building a third party, what are your thoughts on independent parties? Like the Green Party. Is it effective, impactful? Give us some feedback on it.

DHORUBA: Over fifty years ago in Gary, Indiana, we convened the Black Convention to formulate a Black political party. It was the Jesse Jacksons and the so-called Negroes who would later populate the Black Caucus in Congress. They were the ones who said this was pretty premature. That we should exercise. That it was too early for us to leave the Democratic Party. That we need to exercise whatever power we can within a Democratic Party, in a Constitutional party and then we can transform it. Before that, we were always voting for the lesser of two evils.

KALONJI: So basically, it was co-opted.

DHORUBA: Oh, yes, they side-tracked it, and so the lesser of two evils is still evil. The idea of a third political party could never take off, but actually the third political party is a Black political party or, what I would say, a multiracial political party. A rainbow coalition that would evolve into a political party with Black leadership, with Third World leadership, with working-class leadership that would be a dynamic factor right now in the US because of the influence of corporate money and of white males with guns in the electoral process. I mean, we have senators right now . . . we got Lauren Boebert, she's posed up on the podcast with AK47s behind her, her whole family is around a Christmas tree with AR15s and stuff. The other one is talking about she's going to Congress strapped. This is some white women who are feeling themselves.

What do we have? We got sisters singing about we need to trust in Jesus. We need to get a new civil rights bill, and we're going to march across the Pettus Bridge. We're going to remember Martin. This is what we got, and back in the day, man, I know my mama would have slapped the taste out of these white women's mouths talking this yit-yat shit in front of her.

KALONJI: I think that's the thing, too, what you're talking about, those who will get physical—for a lack of a better word—they're not allowed near the podium, or damn near the building itself, because they know they're not going along with whatever is politically correct. They came for the blood, and that is just like you're saying.

DHORUBA: You have to have people, any people that want liberation they have to have a segment of their society that is willing to step forward to protect the integrity of their community, this is about the social, political, and economic integrity of our community. As long as the whites supremacists know that they could victimize us, and we have no redress except through their system of accountability, then they will run amok—and they have run amok—and they will do whatever they want to.

We do have a human right to self-defense, and that hasn't been taken from us by the Constitution of the United States. In fact, it's been enshrined in the Constitution of the United States, but we have been told that we cannot win by exercising our right to self-defense—that we cannot organize ourselves into well-regulated militias in our community under the color of law and win. We have people in our community who are afraid of freedom. They are afraid of the uncertainty that freedom has, and they're comfortable with the certainty of oppression. At least they know, we can't do this and we can't do that, so we have to get out and demonstrate.

What people often still misunderstand about the BPP—which started out as the Black Panther Party for Self-Defense—is that its use of the gun grew out of a grassroots need to put the police in check in Oakland, California at that historical moment in 1967. Oakland had come into being as a consequence of World War II, when many Black workers from the South went to cities like Richmond and Oakland in the Bay Area looking for jobs. They were working for the Navy, loading ships, fighting the war in the Pacific. They settled there, and these cities became predominantly Black. But that also attracted these crackers, these rednecks from Texas and Louisiana, who by-and-large came looking for jobs themselves and wound up in law enforcement. They had the same racist redneck attitude towards Black people in California that they had in Louisiana, in Texas, and in Arkansas, etc. The policing was very racist and very arbitrary.

The Black Panther Party, which was founded by Bobby Seale and Huey P. Newton, who were law students at Merritt College, came together, historically, in a moment that Black people were being harassed by the police. They were being stopped and they were being killed.

In one spot, children were getting run over because there's no stoplight at this intersection. People would zoom into that intersection recklessly, and a number of young kids were killed on the way to school and in that area. The BPP decided that they were going to be the traffic cops in that area. Not only that, but Huey also realized that the lawbook permitted Black people certain constitutional rights, certain legal rights that the Black folks were not aware of. Huey decided that they would observe the police on their patrols and in their comings and goings in the Black community. Whenever they pulled over someone, Huey would stand the legal distance away and advised the brother about his constitutional rights and say, "Brother, you don't have to answer that question. Ask the officer, could you go," and the police hated this.

The police couldn't do much about it because Huey had a shotgun, and Bobby had a .45. The Forte brothers were strapped with carbines and M1's standing around looking appropriately threatening.[9] You know how white folks get, they could see a little kid, thirteen and fourteen years old, and feel like, he's seven feet tall, and their lives are in imminent danger. . . . These actions disturbed the law enforcement at this time, but there wasn't much they could do about it because Huey was within the parameters of the law. Now, the purpose of the gun was to show Black folks that they had the right to stand up for their rights and they didn't have to be abused by someone with a blue costume on and a badge telling them what to do.

This began to significantly resonate in the Black community, and the BPP's ranks expanded in Oakland and in the Bay Area. They had to do something about this, the state legislature had to do

---

9 Reggie and Sherwin Forte were founding members of the Black Panther Party who joined the neighborhood patrols with Bobby Seale and Huey P. Newton as highschoolers.

something about this. They tried to pass a law, a no-open-carry law in California, which up until that point was open carry. That was the law that Huey availed himself of.

The NRA, the National Rifle Association, did not support the BPP's opposition to this law as they support all so-called anti-Second Amendment legislation. They did not oppose that. In fact, they joined with the state on this law in order to disarm the Panthers and to disarm Black people, or disavow them, or dissuade them from the notion that they had a right to bear arms, and they had a right to defend themselves, even against police aggression.

The gun was not used to say that we were going to march to Washington, DC and shoot our way into the White House, and overthrow the US government. Although that would have been cool, too. We weren't with that. We were trying to get Black people to understand that they had a right to self-defense, and they had a right to defend themselves. The Panther Party's ideology has always, consistently, been clear about this.

That's what led to us calling for a united front, a National Front Against Fascism, and setting up committees against fascism in each city and put community control of police, decentralization of law enforcement, and public safety on the electoral ballot. We put that on the ballot in California. We put that on the ballot in New York. We put that on the ballot in Boston. We put that on the ballot in many places where Black people voting were a majority in the community. It was this that scared the police the most.

When people focus on the breakfast program and the health clinics, they fail to make a distinction between that and armed propaganda. The breakfast program, although it concretely fed children, although it concretely had a purpose that was social and beneficial immediately, reflected the idea and the notion that together we could feed ourselves. Together we could take our institutions and service our own needs. The breakfast program was meant to do that, and the gun was meant to defend these programs. The gun was to say that we need to control law enforcement in our own community.

The laws that permit us to carry weapons. We should organize gun clubs, we should organize our communities with legal weapons in order to stop the knuckleheads running around in the community shooting and maiming our people and in order to curtail racist law enforcement and police brutality in our community. The gun was never seen as a means. The gun, basically, was looked upon as an instrument to galvanize, revolutionize, and educate Black people. We use Mao Zedong's phrase that, "Political power grows out of the barrel of a gun."

A poll conducted in 1969 amongst Black people found that almost two-thirds of the respondents admired the BPP and another poll published by *TIME* magazine the following year revealed that almost two million Black Americans considered themselves to be revolutionaries. These results shocked the establishment. When they asked people about that choice, the response was that out of all the organizations advocating for Black people like the NAACP and the SCLC, the one they respected the most was the BPP. The people knew that the police were out to get them because they stood up for Black people. Black folks are not stupid. They know who stands for them and who doesn't.

But because of mass media, this leadership class, and these soft-shoe Negroes that we have in political office today, we have been convinced that any type of militant, or revolutionary ideology, or organization, is somehow negative, self-defeating, and can't succeed in America. The majority of Americans—besides being the dumbest population on the planet—the majority of Americans haven't got a clue about what socialism really means. They haven't got a clue. This is a consequence of the Cold War.

That's one of the reasons why our talk today about the murder of Fred Hampton and how it coincides with the rise of the Black capitalists and opportunists in the minstrel class is very important.

Someone pointed out to me, how the gangbanging history of the '70s has created tribes in the Black community, where you have third and fourth and fifth generation Bloods and Crips. Me, when I was growing up and I was in an urban street set, we stopped gang-banging at sixteen. If you were gangbanging after that, something was the matter with you.. After sixteen, you're supposed to be a hustler, if you walked the streets. You're supposed to be a player. You ain't supposed to be running around with your hat on backwards shooting people and shit. You're supposed to have been slicker than that. At least you'd move to being a thug, another level. I'm just saying, you didn't have a grandfather who was a Crip, and his name was Graveyard so your daddy's name is Little Graveyard and your name is Young Graveyard.

We have to deal with the fact that we have Negroes running the plantation down here in Georgia. That's what it is. Negroes are running the plantation in Baltimore. They running the plantation in Georgia and they running the plantation in Chicago. We need to have grassroots leadership that is responsible to the grassroots, is responsive to Black people. That's what I want to say in the season of the switch. When we talk about something like a third political party, we're talking about mobilizing the forces in the United States that will soon be the majority in this country. The demographics in this country are showing that white, Christian males are soon going to go the way of the buffalo.

KALONJI: Extinct.

DHORUBA: You see, the US will be a multi-racial and multi-ethnic society. What is the role of Black people in this? People don't understand that a third political party is something that has to be organized—given the history of oppression in this country—by the marginalized, by working people, by poor people. They have to represent these constituents.

When we look at something like the Green Party that evolved over the decade or so. It came out of progressive anti-war sentiments, anti-fossil fuel sentiments. It came from progressive white activists to form a third political party, and it has had a hard time even getting on the ballot in many states, but it's persevered. The Green Party was always a progressive movement, was always attempting to try to offer up a different viewpoint, a different view, and a different a strategic vision of politics in America. It was always anti-fossil fuels, it was pro-environmental, it was antiracist, it was working-class, but the Green Party could never take off like it did in Europe, because here in the US you have the Electoral College system.

The Electoral College system was created to make sure that the masses of people could never take the property, and the wealth, and the political clout of those who have power and property. This is why you could have a majority of people vote for one candidate, win the popular vote, and still have a minority elect the actual president through the Electoral College system. In fact, Donald Trump and his minions were attempting to hijack the last election using a weakness of the Electoral College system. We need to understand that there's no true democracy in America with the Electoral College system. Winner takes all.

In Europe, the Green Party can be a large party, and they might just get 15 percent of the vote, which guarantees them a voice in the opposition in parliaments. They're not out of it, they have influence. In fact, a party might win the elections with 35 percent of the vote, another party gets 15 percent, and yet another party that gets 20, then the party that won has to form a coalition with these other parties, and make concessions to these other parties. For instance, the minister of women's affairs might come from the Green Party, the minister of transportation might come from the social democrats. Even though the party that won the elections might have been a center or right-wing party. It has to have a coalition, but in America it's not like that.

In the Electoral College system, with electoral votes, winner takes all. That's how a buffoon like Donald Trump, a con man like Donald Trump, an idiot like Donald Trump, a dumb-ass white boy, could become the commander-in-chief for the United States Military and the President of the United States. To the shame of white folks. White folks can't get over the fact that they elected this idiot.

KALONJI: I'm still stunned because we lived in that area, that region where he was a buffoon for decades before he became president.

DHORUBA: Everybody knew.

KALONJI: I think that the thing that's closest to him, we would have never thought that Al Sharpton would have been taken seriously, just like Donald Trump. Because we always knew Sharpton was a bobble head. Before he was a bobble head, we knew that he was a clown. We couldn't see down the barrel of time to say that Al Sharpton would be taken serious amongst the masses either. I blame it on New York. I blame it on you brothers up in the Bronx. [Laughs.]

DHORUBA: You could blame it on the boogie if you want to. Sharpton made it clear he was about leadership by victimhood.

KALONJI: He was clear. He took Jesse's place.

DHORUBA: If you notice his so-called last march on Washington that he conducted. He had every relative of almost every Black person that was murdered by the police up on the podium. This is leadership by victimhood. We had victims, these are victims, and these are families that lost their loved ones to the violence of the white supremacist racist police state. All they could get is a settlement. You might get one or two convictions, or the police get dismissed, but basically there was no accountability.

It were these people that were put forward. They're on the radio programs, they're telling people, "We understand that people should come out, and we should wait for the system to do its course, but let's not have no violence, let's not burn down anything." They determined the parameters of the issue, and the debate is about the victim. George Floyd was the victim of wanton police murder. He wasn't a political activist when he was murdered. His family didn't have an ounce of politics and was thinking nothing about getting involved in any type of movement. He was a victim.

We should be outraged by his murder, by all means. We should have empathy, sympathy and solidarity with his family, but his family sentiments and lack of politics shouldn't direct the dynamics of our movement. Victims don't lead movements. Once they step up to become a revolutionary or become an activist, they're no longer victims.

KALONJI: That's right.

DHORUBA: Victims are only people who remain victims, and that's where the Sharptons, and all of these, the Crumps. . . . When was the last time Ben Crump won a case? He has never won a case. All he gets are settlements. You see what I'm saying? All he gets are settlements. He never won a case.

The reason why they can say something like in the Ahmaud Arbery case, where these crackers were convicted. It was obvious to a doughnut, to a duck, that they hunted this man down and killed him. The cracker that filmed it, he was filming it to show that they were right.

KALONJI: They did what they did to Trayvon. The same thing.

DHORUBA: When we look at that, we knew that was coming, that a conviction was coming. It was an almost all-white jury. I think they had one Black person on the jury that came back with the conviction. The first thing Sharpton says at the press conference, "This is a monumental victory because it shows that white people can come to the conclusion that a Black person was murdered unjustly by a racist." Come on, man.

Then, you had the Rittenhouse situation where a white boy traveled across state lines with an illegal weapon and killed two white protesters. These were white folks in solidarity with Black people. Then, you would have certain elements of supposedly woke folks talking about, "Well, this white boy killed other white boys." You see what I'm saying?

Whereas I know from my experience that some of my strongest comrades in alliance with us were white comrades. Some of them were even LGBTQ white comrades back in the '60s. They were on the frontline. Who were the Weathermen?[10] Who were the FALN?[11] They weren't all pitch-black. They weren't the BLA. We had white folks who took the idea and the notion of liberation and working-class freedom and independence of Black people seriously. These were our allies, they were solid allies.

We need to understand that although white supremacy is the overarching context of capitalism in this society, that this society is a capitalist society with definite class interests and class divisions that we have to pay attention to. It's very important that if we talk about a third political party, we have to talk about a third political party that's led by the most radical segment of society, the most oppressed segment of society, and that would be people of African ancestry and poor people.

When we look at the people's campaign led by Reverend Barber, this is a campaign that includes masses of working-class people, Indigenous people, poor people, all types of people in this campaign to change the moral and ethical basis in America.[12] This is an

---

10 A white direct action, underground guerrilla combat organization that emerged in the 1960s in opposition to the Vietnam War and white supremacy. See Dan Berger, *Outlaws of America: The Weather Underground and the Politics of Solidarity* (Oakland, CA: AK Press, 2006).

11 Fuerzas Armadas de Liberación Nacional Puertorriqueña, an armed guerrilla movement fighting for Puerto Rican liberation and self-determination.

12 See Poor People's Campaign: A National Call for a Moral Revival, https://www.poorpeoplescampaign.org.

organization and a poor people's campaign that took up where Dr. King left off. Now, we know that when Dr. King was killed, Jesse Jackson, John Lewis and all these niggas, they fled. They left the Poor People's Campaign and pursued their own political careers. When Martin and Malcolm were killed, it created a whole generation of opportunists and cowards who the system then began to elevate and relate to.

We wound up with them, instead of a third political party. Martin Luther King, Jr. died in Memphis, Tennessee, fighting for the rights of garbage men. Garbage men, sanitation workers. When we understand that, we understand the basis for a third political party are poor, working-class, marginalized people of all ethnic backgrounds, and all racial backgrounds. That we have one thing in common, that we have to be anticapitalist corporate elite. We have to build a system that caters to working-class people and ordinary people. Not a system that's based on our ability to consume and go into debt.

A third political party is still not being talked about. The Green Party in the United States is always going to be somewhat limited in its ability to mobilize people because the Electoral College system is a winner take all system. It's even hard for them to get on the ballot in certain cities, in certain places. We don't have a democracy in America, we have democratic fascism. That's what we have, we have a garrison state that's run by white men with guns, and we have a political system of democratic fascism.

KALONJI: Amen. Anyway, comrade, love you man, stay on point. We're going to win in spite of ourselves. Long live Dr. Mutulu. Free all political prisoners. Free Imam Jamil. Free Mumia, Veronza,[13] Ruchelle, Dr. Joy Powell, and all of those folks who have been fighting on behalf of our people, and those who have been forgotten.

DHORUBA: Right on! Peace, Brother.

---

13 Veronza Bowers, Jr. is a former member of the Black Panther Party sentenced to life imprisonment. He was released on May 7, 2024. See the Jericho Movement, https://www.thejerichomovement.com/profile/bowers-veronza.

2

TO BE BLACK IS NECESSARY, BUT IT AIN'T SUFFICIENT

On Black encapsulation and appropriation

"There's no loyalty among pork-chop nationalists."

KALONJI: What's good with you?

DHORUBA: Like I said, it's like fighting fire with a feather. It's looking pretty good, man. [I want to give] a shout-out to Black Power Media and the enormous contribution they made. They did a marathon to raise funds for my medical and related treatment and support. The fundraising went off the chain. I was surprised, and I'm pleasantly surprised. I just want to give a thankful thank you to all the people that contributed, known and unknown.

I really appreciate it. I don't know. I don't have words to really express it, but it was very gratifying to know that people came forward to deal with my situation, especially when we have so many comrades that are passing. They're in their senior years, in the winter of their lives, and many of them don't have the type of support, material and political support that younger generation, that our comrades and young folks should be able to provide.

All you guys, I really appreciate it. I don't want to take up more time with that, but I just want folks to know that I'm really appreciative, and I hope to stay in the fight.

KALONJI: Can you talk about how to navigate the challenges of the Black community today and the real kind of power we need to face our situation?

DHORUBA: Today, when we talk about how we deal with our situation as Black people in the US around issues of immigration, economic control in our community, and the use of political power in our community it all comes down to us understanding our role as working people and the role that we play as consumers. Jared Ball and his constant attempts to show how capitalism and consumerism has faked us into believing that buying power is political power or social power should be bearing fruit now, because we need to understand that Black faces in high places of course do not represent the interests of Black people if these Black faces in high places are trying to survive or trying to use reformism in order for themselves to survive. Like, when we make asinine statements such as "defund the police" rather than the decentralization and community control of public safety. The latter recognizes that we do have power on a local level, that we do have political power on a local level. The Republicans and the right wing realized that all politics is local, that's why they're taking over community school boards and putting their own local legislators in place to promote and protect their strategic visions.

On the other hand, we have our "misleaders" who are selling us out with movements that are led by victimhood. We have leadership by victimhood. We're led by the victims of police brutality. They're the ones that determine the nature of our resistance. You see we have the pork-chop preachers and reformers and these Negroes in the Congressional Black Caucus who are silent when US bombings and killings and drone attacks in Africa and across the Middle East. They are loudly proclaiming their solidarity with the government in its murder of Palestinians, in its support of the European settler-state of Israel, in support of US sanctions against Venezuela, sanctions against Cuba, sanctions against anybody that threatens the hegemonic ambitions of the US.

So, we have these Negro representatives sitting in Washington, who are carrying out basically an international form of gentrification, supporting international gentrification—if you want to use that term—that's being unwound and initiated and used in our communities every day. We know there is gentrification going on in every Black domestic colony in America whether it's Chicago, New York, the Bay Area. Gentrification is an engine. It's a result of the concentration of money and power in corporate real estate interests in the US.

KALONJI: That was a real nice term for a brutal reality. It was nice of you to say "international gentrification." You know that? [Laughs.]

DHORUBA: I lived in Ghana. They put up roadblocks at night in Ghana, to check people and stuff like this, it's very regimented. When you look at the equipment of the police, they have the exact same bulletproof vests—I mean, they might have the first generation—but all of their equipment is made in the US. Their weapons are made in the US, their flak jackets . . . everything they're wearing. They look like US soldiers or police, they just have a Ghanaian flag on their shoulder. You could exchange it for an American flag and you wouldn't be able to tell the difference just looking at them.

We need to understand that America has dominated and imposed its own brand of law enforcement around the world when we talk about something like gun control or the US arms industry. The US arms industry is the largest on the planet, and this industry is lily-white. When we ask ourselves, "Who's making these missiles?" It's Raytheon. "Who's making these fighter planes?" It's Boeing, McDonnell Douglas, Lockheed Martin. It's these corporations. Then we look around in the Black community: there's no Raytheon plants in Harlem, in New York, in Chicago. So, who's making all of this? There are no arms manufacturing plants in the Black community and Black areas. None. Black folks don't make drones, they don't make rockets, they don't make anti-tanks guns, they don't make missiles, they don't make any of these things. We are on the receiving end of these things. This is a major source of finance and wealth for the US, and it's no coincidence that the government could pass a multibillion-dollar military budget, but quibble over universal health care and fight over debt forgiveness for students. Anything that benefits the ordinary working-class consumer is a struggle. It's something that has to be debated, but the military and the police, they get it *carte blanche*. They get whatever they want.

Almost every alliance that the US engages in comes with a huge, multibillion-dollar arms contract. Whenever the US enters a treaty, or enters a relationship, economic or political, with a Third World country, with a poor country, with other countries, especially in Africa, it's always about how the US can enhance its sales of arms and weaponry. Recently, the US and the United Arab Emirates agreed on a $23 billion arms deal, in exchange for the UAE recognizing the legitimacy of the European settler state of Israel. Now, how is it connected to us in the diaspora? The connections are several. The foremost connection of course is economics. That the US government and the US economy thrives and profits from war—either from the threat of war or from actual wars. For the opportunists among the Black capitalist and Black entrepreneur class: where's your arms industry? You want a seat at the table, how come you don't get part of this $23 billion arms deal that's been cut with the UAE, or the many hundreds of other deals that have been made.

The arms industry in America is lily-white for a reason. That's the first thing. The political representation of the arms industry is the National Rifle Association. The gun manufacturers' lobby. Now, what is our relationship with the gun manufacturing lobby? We are on Capitol Hill lobbying for more stringent regulations for gun ownership, and the arms manufacturers who are profiting from the multibillion-dollar deal with the UAE are the same ones who we're fighting against here about gun ownership regulations.

How the US carries out its foreign policy and therefore, how it uses its arms industry to finance itself and to arm repressive regimes around the country that end up oppressing African people, people of color, is very significant. Our elected officials on Capitol Hill in the Congressional Black Caucus are absent without leave whenever it comes to talking about US foreign policies initiatives in Africa and in the Middle East.

Many things are different now than they were in the '60s. The Black Panther Party and most of the left movements back then were in solidarity with most of the armed struggles in Africa, the Middle East, and around the world. We were in such strong solidarity that these liberation movements invited our leadership to their liberated territories in their countries. This is why Huey and the members of the central committee went to China and met with Zhou Enlai. This is why we went to the Congo. This is why we sent a delegation to North Korea. This is why we were in solidarity with the PFLP in Palestine. We had support committees here in the US. This type of international solidarity was directly tied into the idea and the notion of resistance to global finance, capitalism, and imperialism. In the US, it's very sad that our elected officials never speak up on behalf of the people of Africa. When was the last time you heard a Black elected official in Washington, DC call out these two pigs in the Sudan who are killing the Sudanese people, decry them and demand that the US government do something with these two idiots? You haven't heard a peep. The Congressional Black Caucus is in line with US foreign policy, step by step, whether it's Haiti, whether it's Africa, or in fact, whether it's the South Bronx.

When Martin Luther King came around to understanding imperialism, capitalism and white supremacy, like Stokely and Malcolm X had, he started talking about American capitalism, saying that he was perhaps "integrating his people into a burning house" and that "the greatest purveyor of violence in the world was the United States." That's when he was assassinated. The minute he was assassinated, all of his psycho fans, all the Negroes, like Jesse James and John Lewis, all of these bootlickers, they all fled and left the campaign against poverty. They fled the Poor People's Campaign and King's commitment to working-class poor people that he died for in Memphis when he went to march for Black sanitation workers. They fled and pursued their own political career. They began to sidetrack Black discontent and ameliorate Black rage. The Congressional Black Caucus became just another cabal of Negro leaders who were bent on pimping success and the notion of the first Black this and the first Black that, measuring success by white supremacist standards.

John Lewis, somebody who has done absolutely nothing, who was motivated by King, has a state funeral attended by former presidents, eulogizing and praising this guy. And the man that he followed, Dr. Martin Luther King, never had a state funeral. We had to fight twenty-five years just to get a state holiday for this man. He never laid in state, because at the end of the day, King was not the type of leader that white people could endorse and say, "Follow him." John Lewis is because he never really did anything.

KALONJI: Right. You're on point. When you talk about the Congressional Black Caucus and these other toothless tigers, should we expect them to speak up for what's going on in the continent when they're not speaking up for what's going on in the local cities, the local blocks that they're on? They don't care about us here.

DHORUBA: By the fickle finger of fate, if we were to launch a national campaign and we had six or seven different cities that were talking about decentralization of police and community control of public safety, most of those individuals in the Congressional Black Caucus would oppose it.

KALONJI: Man, listen. Most of these cats that are calling themselves nationalists would oppose it.

DHORUBA: They're not going to advocate for it. They are the ones that we need to advocate for it. It's the police union that gave them a nod to get elected from the beginning. It's the police union that could cut off their campaign funding. The police union could talk about how they cop haters and they hate police.

Then they going to be on the trail talking about how they don't hate police. They just want even-handed law enforcement. They going to start hemming and hawing. You don't need them Negroes. The fact is that people make it safe for them to come back to their constituents and hold a town hall meeting. They hold a town hall meeting, nobody stands up.

The Haitian minority in the community don't stand up and say, "What did you do in Congress when it came to the US and the UN voting to send troops and UN forces to Haiti? How are you representing the Haitian community in the United States?" You aren't hearing a peep from them. You're hearing nothing out of them. We ain't heard nothing out of the Congressional Black Caucus when they performed a coup on Aristide. We only have heard a little bit when the Haitian refugees were getting beat at the border. A few of them said something. They tried to put it the context of residual racism. We have elected officials and elected intelligentsia that do not mean African people well.

That's the bottom line. They want us to become equal opportunity exploiters. They want to sit at the table so that we can be equal opportunity oppressors, so that we could vote, "Yay, send the troops into the Congo," so that we could say, "Yeah, we want access to cobalt so we can make these batteries and hire Black people in Detroit to work for Tesla." We don't have Black people that go into politics to be the Humpty Dumpty of the political establishment. In other words, a lot of Black activists who wind up becoming elected officials, that becomes their career.

They want to get reelected. They want to finish what they thought they started, so they want another term and another term. Then they want their homeboy if they can't do another term to endorse him, and then he comes in. Or she comes in. What we don't have are Black activists to say, "Man, if they elect me as mayor, when I'm finished with this city, they're going to never be able to put these crackers back in power again. I'm going to decentralize the police by fear. I'm going to make community control by mayoral decree. I'm going to use my influence on the city council and browbeat them so the civilian complaint review boards no longer exist." Now, there are community control boards and public safety boards. In other words, you can do all of these things. Then, if you don't get reelected, it's all good. Let the next mayor try to undo that and see what happens.

Once people taste that power, homeboy come and he going to have a problem trying to dismantle it. It's just like Humpty Dumpty. I call it the Humpty-Dumpty principle.

KALONJI: Listen here, man, on that note with the Humpty-Dumpty principle, [laughs] we're going to definitely get you back on, figure out how to break this egg and scramble it.

DHORUBA: Like I said, it looks bad for the home team, man.

KALONJI: It looks bad for the home team?

DHORUBA: I'm south of Sahara on the eve of Armageddon, bro, ass out. [Laughs.]

KALONJI: While we are talking about terms: the nonprofit social justice movement operating under the guise of Black power, how do we deal with that and how do we differentiate? We're clear that there are "American Negroes" whose sole purpose is to misguide, misdirect, and mislead. We were talking earlier, and one of the things you said that I thought was funny was around pork-chop nationalists. You said "there's no loyalty amongst pork-chop nationalists."

DHORUBA: There's no loyalty among pork-chop nationalists. [Laughs.]

KALONJI: How are we going to deal with that, because I see that as a problem as well. Maybe I'm tripping, maybe I'm getting older and I'm catching an attitude and whatnot. Ladies and gentlemen, Dhoruba is being my therapist tonight! [Laughs.]

DHORUBA: Man, I don't know how I'm your therapist. I lost my mind a long time ago. That's why I'm over here. I'm still looking for it. [They laugh.]

When I say there's no loyalty amongst pork-chop nationalists, I'm referring to those who do not emphasize culture as a revolutionary instrument for liberation, but rather as a return to traditional roots that do not liberate us in real time in the here and now. These are individuals, who appropriate all of the trappings of Blackness and culture. They might have been in back and forth to the continent twenty-nine times. To them, merely the expression of our Africanness is empowering.

Look at Speaker of the House of Representatives, democrat Nancy Pelosi, when she came here to Ghana in 2019 during "The Year of Return," she had kente around and knelt down and held Nana Akufo's hand and basically said, "I apologize for the slave trade. We apologize. Now that we apologize, don't mess with them Chinese no more. Don't mess with them."

Like I said, there's no loyalty among pork-chop nationalists because you'll have another set of pork-chop nationalists who might be messianic in their view, and that's how they practice the pork-chop nationalism. In other words, they say that, "We have a divine mission here." That, "We ourselves are supreme, because we have Black civilization behind us. Once we were kings. Once we were kings and queens." I'll always consider myself trying to be a working-class poor man's hero. Pork-chop nationalists will cut each other's throats, in order to be the one everybody invites to "Kwanzaa" and all the different events. Pork-chop nationalists have no problem with capitalism at all. You could be a pork-chop nationalist and say, "Buy Black." You could be a pork-chop nationalist and just say, "Black art, you should buy Black art and you should do all of these things merely because it's Black."

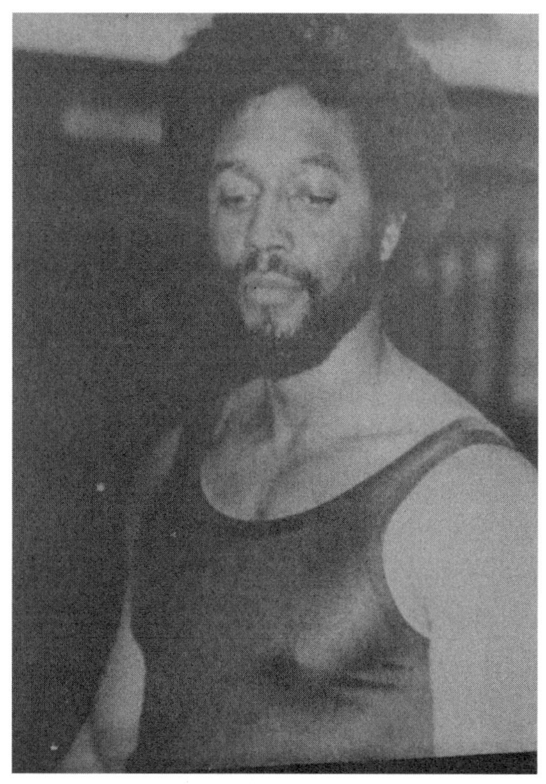

3

THE UNSTOPPABLE POWER OF SELF-DETERMINATION

From "Power to the People" to the Congressional Black Caucus[1]

"We didn't have Facebook. We didn't have computers then. We had Emory Douglas."

DHORUBA: If young people today were to go back and look at the presidential debates in 1960 between Nixon and Kennedy, they would see that both the Democrats and the Republicans were talking about the exact same thing we are talking about today: how America must reassert its leadership in the world, how America must deal with attacks on American sovereignty and American interests abroad. How the US had to have law-and-order industries, how we needed law and order and how Nixon was a law-and-order candidate, like Trump or Clinton today.

We see that these same issues come up generationally over, and over, and over again. Now, why is that? The reason is because of the destruction of the Black Panther Party, and we must understand that the BPP wasn't the only organization that was destroyed by COINTELPRO. By late 1969, early '70, the FBI had already won its repressive war against the left and against the Black Liberation Movement. They had already won it, tactically speaking. They had managed to turn "Power to the People" into the Congressional Black Caucus. Almost every initial member of the Congressional Black Caucus was part of the poverty bill class that LBJ initiated with his war on poverty.

---

1 This conversation is an abridged version of two interviews conducted for Black Power Media on August 1, 2020 and December 4, 2020. The text has been edited for clarity and flow.

We need to understand that this evolved over time. This repression of COINTELPRO is in the institutional memory of white supremacy and they just go back to the playbook. They know that these Black people who are sincere, they can be encapsulated. They can be turned away from any real change because they don't declare themselves an abolitionist movement, they don't declare themselves revolutionary, they don't say that.

They were community organizers. They started out that way. They started getting funding, they decided to run for office, and then the riots and rebellions in the streets made them realize that the government—which was heavily involved in war abroad in Vietnam—was looking bad, and therefore it had to have Black faces in high places. We went from having one or two mayors in a major city in the late 1960s to having dozens of mayors today. In all these cities, the police culture has not changed. In fact, in most of the cities where we saw Black folks being murdered and killed, they have Black mayors and Black police chiefs. This is how they flipped it, because there was no abolitionist movement to abolish white supremacy that came out of the '60s. The nationalist movements were marginalized, the Pan-African movement was demonized and marginalized.

We need to understand that this generational passing on of reactionary politics and white supremacy is exactly what COINTELPRO did. What did COINTELPRO say about Malcom X and Elijah Muhammad and how they could become leaders? They had to in fact make the leaders, all of the Negroes, the soft-shoed n*ggers that they done buried on Capitol Hill, like John Lewis.

They didn't lay Martin Luther King in state. He did one hundred times more to educate and struggle for the rights of African people and Black people than John Lewis ever did. In fact, King was vilified at that time. Same thing with Muhammad Ali, he was vilified at that time. Half of the Negroes who have come out talking about how Ali influenced them and how they love him. These n*ggers that lived back then was hiding in the shadows talking about Ali. "Ali should just go on and fight and keep his mouth shut." We need to understand that this is an evolution that has occurred in de-revolutionizing the movement and making sure that this fear of intimidation was passed on.

What do we always hear these Black bootleg Negroes say when we talking about, we need to defend ourselves? "Oh, you can't beat them with guns. We going to lose. Violence, we going to lose." You're damn sure we going to lose if you start fighting from the beginning. You done lost already. The only ones that were promoted was the soft-shoe niggas like John Lewis, Elijah Cummins and his bootlickers, and people waving bloody T-shirts like Jesse Jackson, and all these folks. These were the ones that were empowered by the system.

Today we see the same thing happening with the Black Lives Matter movement. We see that its elite, its so-called national leadership, gets millions and millions of dollars. It's talking about how Black folks' lives have to be portrayed and how now we see—as one commentator said—when it comes to addressing the needs of Black folks there is always talk about raising everybody's boat. That we are not just for justice for Black people we are for justice for everybody. But they don't say that when it comes to the LGBTQI+, they don't say, "Oh, we can't just pass legislation for LGBTQI+ and gay folks, we have to pass legislation for everybody, heterosexuals too." They don't say that, they only say that when it comes to Black people and there's a reason why.

JARED BALL: Obviously, the outcome of COINTELPRO was to make sure that young Black people were disconnected from these radical traditions. It's not a coincidence that young people are so disconnected. One of the problems I see, is that so much of the conversation around what we're supposed to do is in response to the encapsulation process. The space is taken up by people who don't appreciate these politics or these histories, or don't agree ideologically with the position that you and others have taken.

They are the spokespeople, and even the ones literally telling us of the histories of these people. Like a lot of the more prominent academics and pundits who talked about Kwame Ture or the Black Panthers, they don't agree with these politics. They don't agree with the associated ideas, but they're the more prominent ones. I almost wanted to just say, how do we get more young people to be connected with these histories and to understand them? What do you see as a viable method?

Just the other day, I see T.I. (Tip Harris) go on Roland Martin's show and talk about his plan for reparations from Lloyd's of London, and what his plan for getting Black America some payback from Lloyd's of London. He mentioned that he was in dialogue with Killer Mike and with Robert Smith, the Black billionaire, and other business leaders, but I thought it interesting that he didn't mention that he had just come from a meeting with you, for instance.

DHORUBA: Let me tell you something about that meeting. When T.I. sat down with us, he asked quite clearly, "What is fascism?" We tried to give him a little understanding of it, but the fact that he was sincere and asked meant that, "OK, I didn't really appreciate what fascism is."

Now, we jump to that from this, to him talking about Lloyd's in London and reparations. Now, me, I'm a Pan-African internationalist, and everybody knows where I stand with reparations. What we need is power. What we need is the power number, whatever number it was in the BPP program, I think it was number six. We need the power, or we need the ability to define power for our community. Once we have power, then the discussion about reparations becomes something that can be maintained, that can be financed, that can be turned into boycotts, that could be turned into actions, that could be translated into something concrete that everybody could understand.

Without power, it's rhetoric. Without power, we're saying to white, "Well, y'all owe us some money, when are you going to pay us? If you're not going to pay us, I ain't going to stop demonstrating." "Well, keep demonstrating, nigga, because we ain't paying your Black ass." They don't understand that. Capitalism is confronted with the issue of reparations inherently. That's what it's all about. Reparations is only part and parcel of a redistribution of wealth globally. Now, how the hell you think the forty million Black folks are going to get reparations in America with no power?

Let's just say that willing representatives like John Lewis and the Congressional Black Caucus all agreed to reparations, that we should have them right now. What do you think the effect of that is going to be? Nothing.

JARED: In this moment, that's one of the problems I'm seeing. For instance, I'm not trying to pick on T.I., but it was just a perfectly timed hit that he didn't even acknowledge your involvement, or the ideas that you all would have discussed. He didn't put that on the table.

DHORUBA: The only reason he sat down with us—with Sekou, Bilal, Kalonji, Jamal, and myself—was because he knows Black history. If you notice in the letter, we didn't attack T.I. We didn't attack Killer Mike. We didn't attack none of these people. The reason why we didn't is because we want to try to get Black folks to understand that we're the only people who got entertainers and basketball and football players as our spokespeople. You don't see white people going to a white hockey player asking, "Why do you think the US involvement in this affair in China is wrong? OK, well, what do you think about the Chinese ping pong team making a statement about capitalism?" You see they don't do that. They have their elected officials. They have their spokespeople. They're experts and all these folks to speak about US policy to frame it in the terms of the US, twenty-first century America and democracy, and they frame it all.

We're the only ones who got basketball players and football players trotted out on national television and asked these profound questions. They're not the Harry Belafontes and the Muhammad Alis of the past who deferred to the political leaders of the movement. They got behind them and backed them whenever they needed the demonstration of Kareem Abdul-Jabbar, Jim Brown, whatever the individual politics was.

They all had their individual limitations. Nobody's perfect around here. Nobody's saying that these guys were some types of saints. They weren't. They were imperfect like everybody else, but they had enough principle to understand that they were not the leaders of a movement.

JARED: I'm only saying that to say that their audiences are willfully—in this case it may be inadvertently—disconnected from the traditions and histories that you're trying to connect them to, which we desperately are in need of to advance these struggles beyond the symbolism and the hashtags and all of that.

DHORUBA: I got that, but in your book you debunk the myth of Black buying power. You debunk that. You lay out how capitalism really works here, and what that really represents in terms of so-called wealth. "If we calculated our wealth this way, we'd be the fifth largest nation," and all of that bullshit.

I don't know how many people read Jonathan Livingston Seagull. This was a story of a seagull who loved the art of flight.

Seagulls just fly. It's normal. This seagull, he just loved to fly. He would try all types of tricks. He would try to fly upside down. One time, he got into this zen position. He went up higher than any other seagull ever went before him. When he got up there, these two seagulls, like spirits, flew right next to him. Everything he did, they did. He'd never seen these seagulls before. Then one of the seagulls said to him, "Jonathan, you are trying to perfect the art of flight. You are trying to reach your highest possibility of who you are as a seagull, but just remember this, the bird that flies the highest sees the most."

Now, bringing that back to somebody like T.I., he now doesn't have to sling no yayo in the streets. T.I. now is the OG of a lot of young people who look up to him right now on the path to success in the industry in the field of entertainment and music. He has mastered his craft and his position to his own benefit, and nobody's knocking that. Because I strongly believe there's a lot of young brothers, illegitimate capitalists, whether they're criminals, entertainers, or whatever, if they were the head of major corporations, they'd be better CEOs than many of the corporation managers that we have today. They just have that skill set. That's how they are. They're built that way, but they just never had the chance or the opportunity to access wealth.

T.I. now understands access to wealth. He sees it. Killer Mike is circulating with people who are trying to co-opt him. He was behind Bernie Sanders for all the right reasons, perhaps. Bernie Sanders was talking about universal health care, free public-school education. Bernie Sanders was talking about shit that was really real, in terms of this capitalist society, and that could not be permitted. We know what happened to him.

Killer Mike was a surrogate. What happened to Killer Mike when he gets knocked out? Bernie Sanders supports Biden. Does Killer Mike support Biden? No, Killer Mike falls back on being Black and having access to people who have power. He's on the mayor's committee, empowerment committee here in Atlanta. All of these Black folks who have come into wealth, whether they're T.I., whether they're Jay-Z, or whatever. Jay-Z went behind Kaepernick and established a relationship with the NFL. Now, entertainers can do the Super Bowl and not worry about being labeled sellouts. "Jay-Z hooked us up. If we know Jay-Z, you're not a sellout."

Jay-Z is sitting up with Warren Buffett and other millionaires talking about how he got rich, how his first record hit, and he did this and that. "The gull who flies the highest sees the most." These guys who have been exposed to wealth, they could see the possibilities that they couldn't see when they was slinging that yayo on the street. They never thought that hip-hop would get them that far. Bernie said that, "We ain't never thought it would take us that far."

You see? We ain't never thought that. Now that they did, now they envision, "Why don't we control shit? Why ain't we doing like the Lloyd's of London? Why ain't we doing this?" But they're all thinking like capitalists. They're not thinking like revolutionaries. They're not thinking like Pan-Africans. They're not thinking like they came from the oppressed people.

Why don't we have a Pan-African refugee and relief agency? The African Union (AU), fifty-five nations, doesn't have a Pan-African relief agency. They have to depend on the Red Cross, the Red Crescent. They got to call Doctors Without Borders. They don't have their own. They don't have it. Do we need the AU to form one? When we say Pan-African, we mean all Black folks. Whether it's the homeless mama in Los Angeles or whether it's the sister that's run out of her own village in the Congo by some armed mercenaries who are smuggling coltan into Uganda, so it can be sold on the market and we can have our iPhones. There's Black kids right now in the Congo digging in the mud at twelve and thirteen years old with a knucklehead standing over them with an AK-47. What they are taking out the ground is going straight into the iPhone, is going straight to these corporations. You see.

Do we have Black billionaires and millionaires out of concern for the uplift of Black people coming together and saying, "Look, let's pool our money. I'll kick in 500 million, you kick in 200, you kick in 50. Together, we got $2.5 billion in capital that we can use in terms of microfinancing farmers and trading that farmed goods to the African stores, African markets here in the US."

Look at all the Asian markets you have now. They are importing foods and produce from where? The Middle East, South America, and Africa and selling it here to the people who come from those regions. If I want to get some good oxtails, if I want to get some good yams and stuff, I'm going to the Asian market because they got it.

My point is, is that the shit that T.I. and them is talking is game because they done rose so high they could see what wealth can do, rather than set it up on their own, they going to say, "Well, they owe us money because they financed the slave trade." If crackers owe you money when you was on the street, if somebody owe you money, you went and got your pistol, roll around it and then knocked on the door and say: "N*gger, I want my money." Why don't you do that to white folks?

JARED: It's funny you said that, because the first thing I was thinking of is the part that I admittedly left out of my book. The part that gets left out of a lot of these arguments is the initial basis for the power that gives Lloyd's of London its ability to do what it does, which starts, of course, with military conquest, colonial conquest, military suppression of a population and a theft of their land and their resources. On top of that, you can institute all the laws and regulations that allow you to set up these insurance scams and permanently invest in the rewards. When you used that example, that to me is the perfect microcosm of part of what is missing from this discussion of power.

DHORUBA: Or they wind up with Jay-Z having a personal relationship with the governor of New York and telling him, "Look man, I'll supply masks for the majority of prisoners in the state of New York." He ain't talking about creating a prison break for the state of New York, funding the national conference of Black lawyers to take down the Rockefeller program and take on the sentencing. He ain't talking about that. He's talking about some other shit.

I'm saying to you, if you came up in the street and you were gangster, why ain't you gangster with these crackers now? You dropping some, "We need to do . . . " and "Why don't you. . . ?" All of these gangsters, like my boy Jazz Hayden and them gangsters in Harlem, they formed a council. These are street thugs, they formed a council, so they wouldn't be shooting and killing each other, and they could regulate whatever drugs they were slinging out there so that they could maintain a profit. That only fell apart when they began to turn on each other. Of course, the enemy had something to do with that. That's when it fell apart.

The idea is, if you could form a consortium to control the drugs in your Black community, why can't you form a consortium to empower Black people internationally and nationally? Why can't you do that? You can't do that because you're not looking at them as your enemy. You're looking at them as potential collaborators, as in potential investors. You want them to give back to you what they stole. If I had stolen your money on the street in the South Bronx, you wouldn't be talking about you want your money, you would have came to take my ass out. If you couldn't find me, you find somebody that was close to me, kidnap them and send them back in pieces to me.

This is the oldest gangster shit you do on the street, but when it comes to white folks, you talking about how they got a moral obligation. White folks ain't going to give you jack unless you stick a gun in their face, and you take it. You got to begin that by controlling the guns in your community. The way you control the guns in your community is you take over the armed agents of the state in your community, and you take their tax, your tax money, and fund the police in your community so they protect you, so that they can protect your interest, so that they protect your property, and you decertify the police unions. You do that by taking them to their court, and saying that these guys are outside of their certification. They are exerting political influence into the Black community, and we want that to stop.

I'm just saying that when T.I. talks about what Lloyd's of London did, we know Standard Chartered got a commission off the slave trade. We know Barclays Bank got their money off the slave trade. We know that most of these insurance companies began with the slave trade. We will go to them now and say, "Look man, because you redline housing and we can't get no housing here, and you all continued all of this and you started all of this when my great-great-great-grandmama was a slave, and I want my reparation." That's not how you do that when you're gangster. What happened on that gangster shit you've been talking about? What happened?

JARED: Even for me, as someone who was not a gangster, never was a gangster, to me, the political equivalent of what I hear you say is to organize movements that address themselves to achieving political power. That, to me, is the politically gangster move as opposed to individual claims, arrangements with billionaire business people to get reparations.

DHORUBA: We need to understand that institutions like Standard Chartered Bank, Barclays Bank, and others all got rich off the chattel slave trade. Let's not get this shit twisted, OK? Whenever there's been a decline in human rights, whenever there's been a tragedy, finance capital has always made a profit from it. Always. Out of the Holocaust, out of the murder of millions and millions of people in Europe—Black people, Roma people, not just Jews, but also political dissidents, mainly communists and socialists, OK? Out of this came what? Came the Marshall Plan, the reinvigoration of Europe to what we have today. Out of that Holocaust came the state of Israel, a European settler colonial state, a Zionist state. Zionism went from an ideology of rich Jews in Europe to the ideology of a national security state in the middle of the Middle East.

I want to talk about the lessons to be learned from the BPP that this generation has never been in touch with. We have to understand encapsulation. Encapsulation is the strategy that's employed by the powerful to destroy, to divert, and to dilute movements. It's a very simple strategy. Whenever repressive regimes, governments, and people in power are faced with resistance from oppressed people, from the underclass, from people who they exploit and dominate, they have certain strategies and tactics that they use. One of the tactics that they have, is to encapsulate the most potentially militant segment of those people and move them away from their understanding of their own history. Their own radical tradition. Then, coupled with that is the brute physical removal of leaders that can transmit that type of history and vision.

Besides killing the Malcolm Xs and running Black folks who talked about Black people defending themselves into exile, and aside from killing Black civil rights leaders and Black activists, the objective of the ones holding power was also to co-opt this militancy and encapsulate it. Direct it into avenues of reform and avenues of protest that they could manage. If you listen to Malcolm's speech about the original idea to march on Washington, it was supposed to be more like Black folks' version of January 6. Then it became marching down and singing, "We Shall Overcome," and sitting around the pond to listening to speeches. Which is not to say that that event lacks historical significance. At that particular time, it was a historically significant event, but it was an event that was encapsulated because of so-called potential to shut down the seat of government. That would have been the objective of the most militant workers and activists at that time: to march on Washington and make them recognize our power. Make them recognize that we were people who deserved to have our own self-determination and that if we weren't going to get the type of treatment and the type of services, jobs, and rights that we deserved, then we were going to shut down the government.

That had to be sidetracked. That was encapsulated. You had the Urban League and the NAACP. You had the integrationists in the South who had been fighting and dying for basic rights and everything. You had them put at the head. Malcolm talks about it better than me. We should go listen to Malcolm's speech. I think it was the "Ballot or the Bullet." That strategy is taken in every revolutionary struggle around the world.

Not only do you have to kill the Amilcar Cabrals or the Eduardo Mondlanes. Not only do you have to kill the Patrice Lumumbas, but you have to reconfigure their whole idea of nationhood. You have to reconfigure their whole idea of who they were as a people to make it conform to the neocolonial construct. And they did that with us.

You have to kill the leaders of the revolutionary movement so that they don't pass on their information, their knowledge, and their experience to another generation. This is why, when we see where revolutionary nationalist movements were successful, the people that were revolutionaries, whether they were the Viet Cong in Vietnam, whether they were Frelimo in Mozambique, whether they were PAIGC in Guinea-Bissau, they didn't get the message that they were supposed to lose. They didn't get that memo.

Encapsulation means that you take a movement, or you take an idea, or you take the people who struggle for freedom and you encapsulate it with the type of leaders, with the type of issues so that those people who want to become part of this movement join this organization thinking they're going to achieve these things, when in fact, they have been dead-ended. They're not going to achieve any of these things.

A good contemporary example of this, before Ferguson, was the New Black Panther Party. They were encapsulating the organization. Their purpose was to take the history and the radical tradition of the original Black Panther Party and reinvent it with dogma and with narrow nationalist ideology and an infantile understanding of class, put on black berets, black leather jackets, march around with guns, and people will say, "Oh, this is the Black Panther Party." You have a whole generation that grew up for the past fifteen years that didn't know the original BPP ever existed. They didn't even know what the Ten Point Program was. All they knew was Zulu Shabazz, and these other Negroes that were fronting and running around with guns and boots talking about how white people were the devil. They were using the same old messianic ideology of the Nation of Islam because that's where it came from. But that wasn't the original New Black Panther Party. It came out of Texas, and it did not have that ideology.

It was only when these refugees, so to speak, from the Nation of Islam, took over, that they were able to take the name of the Black Panthers, the imagery of the Black Panthers, and redefine it and reorganize it and refocus it so that it became meaningless. It became just posturing. It became rhetoric. The ideology now became a nationalism that could be easily refuted by facts. If you notice, they had no history. They had no attachment to any radical movements from the past. In fact, they condemned all of the radical movements of the past as being inadequate, bogus, and fake.

Now, we ask ourselves: where is the New Black Panther Party today? It doesn't exist. You haven't seen it on the streets. You haven't seen it in Seattle. You haven't seen it in Portland. You haven't seen it in any of these areas where people have taken them to the streets and outrageous outrage against the injustice of systemic racism. It doesn't exist. That was the purpose of it for fifteen years, to make sure that when people took to the streets this time, they did not have the historical and the radical tradition of the Black Panther Party to actually draw on and develop from that point forward.

We need to understand that encapsulation doesn't just mean taking over an organization and misdirecting it, encapsulation means taking over a people's movement and their historical perception of themselves and redirecting it. People will tell us that our right to vote is what we're in the streets fighting for. Why are we fighting for the right to vote? Black folks have never fought for the right to vote. They fought for the right to be empowered, and voting was a mechanism and a means towards that end. If we could have got empowered without voting, we would've done it, but we know from Tulsa that that was impossible.

Do we hear Black folks today saying taxation is tyranny? No. Not one knucklehead in the Congressional Black Caucus is saying that, "If you're not going to supply the Black community with A, B, C and D in terms of health care, we not going to pay taxes because tax without representation is tyranny."

White folks threw all the tea that Britain had into Boston Harbor because they believed that you can't tax us if we can't represent ourselves. Well, why don't we have that attitude? We're getting taxed, but we don't have housing. We don't have adequate healthcare. They tell them, "Oh, sign up for the census because that's going to determine the number of resources that is going to come to your community." How's that going to determine anything when we have the Republicans and the right gerrymandering our district so our census numbers really don't add up to anything? They gerrymandered themselves into a corner because although they gerrymandered these districts to break up our ability to vote as core Democrats or anti-conservatives or whatever you want to say. They also broke up the district, so if we went to the electoral polls tomorrow and put a referendum for decentralization of police on the ballot, in most of these cities where we are majority, we will probably win that referendum. That means that we could control law enforcement in our community, because in America we don't have a national police force—this is what I meant by the "Frankenstein of fascism." Trump realizes this, and this is why he sent marshals into Seattle and into Portland, because he doesn't have a national police force to take the streets back the way he wants. An authoritarian figure cannot operate without the national police force. Of course, here we have quite the Frankenstein version of that. We have two political parties that act in that fashion for that purpose, but they don't even have a national police force.

The policing in America is on the local, state, county, and municipal level. All police departments have local charters and we could change those, which means that those tax dollars that go to the PBA funds and go to racist policing, could also come to us if we control the police. Now, we go in the cities with mayors and a city manager, a type of structure that appoints the police chief. They put their own political appointee, and of course, he's susceptible to the political pressure of the unions. You never have a Black politician, Black or white, who stands up and doesn't try to make like he's pro-law enforcement in order to get the unions' endorsement. Why would you want the unions endorsement when the union doesn't represent working-class people?

After 9/11, the enemy, the opposition, the corporate rich tried to establish a national police force with Homeland Security. That didn't work. If we look how these federal agents are being used, they're being used to quash dissent. Law enforcement's job is to protect the rich, to guard property rights over human rights, and to enforce the status quo.

If we're talking about the real deal, then we're talking about the Black community controlling public safety. We've got to look at public safety as something more than the police. It's not just the police. It's healthcare. It's sanitation. It's education. It's all these different aspects go to make up the public health of the community. Public safety is a concern of all people in the community. If we don't control public safety, who does? Who determines what's safe for us, and what's not safe for us, if we don't? When we talk about defunding the police, we're not talking about taking a bit of funds that's allocated through the present system to the police, no. We're rethinking law enforcement completely where property rights don't supersede human rights, where the police are not occupiers in our community. In fact, the police ought to live in our community.

Why is it that the police have been quiet about white supremacy and systemic racism in the police department, only filing occasional suits when they feel discriminated against? Why is it that Black cops in the police establishment always want their own union? If the union really represented all the police, why is there need for a Black union? And for a Puerto Rican union? Because the police unions do not represent the interest of even the police that's working there. They represent the interest of the corporation and the status quo that they invest all of that money in. Where does the police union money go? Who did it invest in? Which stocks do they put it in? Why is gun safety such an issue? Because the law enforcement establishment, the military establishment and the arms industry are like one. America is the number one purveyor of arms on the planet. Who trains most of the police departments on the planet? Americans. Who are their major crime partners? Israelis. The whole history of the unions in the Americas organizing and training fascism, death squads in South America for decades.

If we're talking about something as straightforward as controlling the police, it's very simple. This is not rocket science. We know how the police evolved in the US. We know how they evolved from the days of slavery to the urbanizations of certain centers, and building the industrial age. We know about the gangs in New York being organized by that cracker, "Boss Tweed." All of these guys in Chicago and all. This is why the police departments in Chicago, in New York, in Boston, and in Philadelphia were predominantly Irish. There was a reason for that.

We got to go more into history to see why was that. Why weren't the Black folks working around when they were forming the police department? They came out of street gangs in the urban areas. Now, we got street gangs banging in the Black community, and what are we talking about? We don't talk about making them responsible in our community and organizing them into a self-defense force for our community. No, we talking about the fact that we've got to call the cops because we're killing each other. They're killing each other because you let the enemy define the parameters of the issue. Power is the ability to define phenomena.

We see now how to gerrymander districts; to do it on the state, municipal, and township level. This is how they steal our power from us. We not only have to fight in the electoral arena, we have to take control of these institutions on the state and the local level. We have to transform those institutions so that they genuinely reflect our interests. As long as the enemy has a monopoly on violence, as long as the political instruments of power of white supremacy are militarized, we have to organize ourselves to defend ourselves against this.

We could see that with the historic rise of white militias, the Proud Boys and the Second Amendment crew, and all of these folks that ran out of guns in the white community because they bought them all up. In the Black community, the only way we can buy a gun is out of the trunk of a car, in the hood. We haven't established the civil use of firearms to protect our communities, to protect our families, and to control law enforcement policies in our community. In fact, we have stop-and-frisk, which historically has given most Black people criminal records, so they could not legally own arms.

We don't have a Black gun culture other than the street gun culture with gangbangers and gangsters who kill innocent people, who terrorize our community, which in turn the police use to rationalize their treatment of Black people and the Black community, and their policing policies.

If we control the law enforcement policies in our community, you couldn't believe that when somebody calls 911 for a domestic dispute, a white boy with a gun is not going to show up to resolve the dispute. Somebody else is going to show up when we call 911. To deal with that dispute, to deal with it on a whole bunch of different levels other than the use of physical force and violence.

It's true that these young people should reimagine law enforcement. They should talk about defunding the police, but they should have to understand that to reimagine law enforcement and to defund the police means you have to politically empower your community. If you don't politically empower your community, all your imaginations are nothing but dreaming out of season, its nothing but a dream. They're asleep, and they claim to be woke. Now, we really have to understand what that means, we have to take power over our own communities.

The reason why I quoted about power being the ability to define phenomena is because once the parameters of a debate are set, then anything that enters into that debate has to deal with the contradictions or questions or the issues within those parameters. When the white supremacist system and the corporate media sets the parameters of the debate, they automatically hamstring us, because our history, our needs as a people transcend these parameters.

I was listening to NPR and they were highlighting a beef between two neoconservatives who were raised in the rural, white Midwest. One of them said that the murder of George Floyd was not racist because he heard that it was personal. That the officer and George Floyd had run-ins before and that he was actually exercising a personal vendetta on George Floyd. I know, you know, and everybody that understands and analyzes racism knows that white supremacy and racism is not a matter of personal ideology, personal choice, or personal feelings. Racism and white supremacy is a system. It's an economic, cultural, and a political system. Individuals may or may not agree with some of the propositions of it, but it's not about individual exercise of power. It's about the parameters of power exercised by the most powerful, elite entities in society. The same way they try to rectify or justify the Civil War and Confederate monuments as being indicative or symbolic of American culture. It was just about the old boys fighting the good fight, losing, and pulling their lives back together from the devastation of the Civil War. It had nothing to do with chattel slavery. It had nothing to do with wage slavery versus chattel slavery, it had nothing to do with where the US was at economically at that point, where cotton agriculture was at versus industrialization. All these things had nothing to do with. It was just about old boys trying to exercise the culture and stuff, which is total bullshit.

When we talk about Black Lives Matter, we have to understand that it's occurring now in this place at this time. The history of Black radicalism of the '60s, the '50s and the '40s behind it is never mentioned. We have to understand what does "Black lives matter" really mean, when anybody could spring up in any city and rightfully take to the streets, and put it on a T-shirt? Then, the press will come out and say, "This is the Black Lives Matter demonstration." Any individual who had asked him, "You are a member of BLM. What's happening with this chapter?" "Well, I started out just now. We're not really a chapter. We are not organized." Everybody gets mysterious. Where do all the millions of dollars go? It's going to a hashtag? It's going to a movement that doesn't exist?

Now we have Black Lives Matter encapsulating the idea and the notion of the Black Liberation Movement. If we look at the history of the merger between the Black Panther Party and SNCC, how it broke up, it's in the COINTELPRO profile. When was last time we heard anybody from the Black Lives Matter movement talk about COINTELPRO? Talk about it and refer to the actual files, which don't exist outside of the FBI? Why? Because the enemy has institutional memory. The state has institutional memory. It's the activists that don't have an attachment to the historical memory, so we reinvent failure.

Black Lives Matter is headed towards encapsulation. It's encapsulating all of this rage, all of this momentum, and it's leading nowhere. It's talking about "divestment." What does "divestment" mean? Divestment of the police department. What will that change? It's talking about "defund." What will defunding the police change? What would actually change?

That's why slogans are so important in a movement. I mean, look at the Vietnamese people, I studied the Vietnamese movement and how they passed it on from one generation to the next. They used to sit down at political education classes in order to determine what slogan should they use for this particular movement in this particular village that the people can latch onto and that the enemy cannot use against them.

Slogans are important. When we said power to the people, the pigs couldn't say power to the pigs. We had already defined racist law enforcement and racist landlords as pigs. We used that imagery, the same type of imagery they use today. We didn't have Facebook. We didn't have computers then. We had Emory Douglas. That was better than any Facebook software, that was better than any AI software. We could portray that your landlord had the head of a pig and flies were buzzing around his head, and he was a victim of some Black poor folks from the house. People could relate to that.

And the enemy had to respond to it. Like in New York, for instance when we talked about community control and decentralization of police. They put up pictures and posters in the subways. Big posters with a white cop with sweat on his face, like he just came out of a fire, holding a Black baby, and the caption underneath would say, "And some would call him a pig." They had to respond to our imagery.

JARED: Thank you very much for doing this, having this conversation. We'll definitely look to have many more with you. As always, because it's clear as day with you, to you we say peace because you're willing to fight for it, like Fred Hampton used to say. Peace to you, Dhoruba, and everybody watching. Thanks for tuning in.

DHORUBA: Thanks again, brother. Peace.

RECOLLECTIONS OF A BLACK REVOLUTIONARY

On Assata Shakur, Angela Davis, and COINTELPRO[1]

"We're only going to be free when we break the political power of the police over the state."

KALONJI: Honored to have today in our midst the cofounder of the Black Liberation Army. A veteran Panther from the New York area, he was framed as one of the lead defendants of the Panther 21 case, which involved folks like Afeni Shakur, who is Tupac's mother, of course, Sekou Odinga, Jamal Joseph, and a number of other folks, to name a few.

That case was beat and thrown out, and about six days later, Dhoruba Bin Wahad was framed again in a case in which he served nineteen years. Through the work of his lawyers, they were forced to release him because they found out that the FBI had pulled a fake move on the whole thing.

I want you to stand up and give our good brother, Dhoruba Bin Wahad, a round of applause. How you feeling, brother?

DHORUBA: Peace.

KALONJI: The sister Zahra was running off what folks know of Assata, the case, the basics of what was going on. What we want to do is we want to allow the people the opportunity to get a better picture of who she is, what her purpose was, and why the situation

---

1 This interview was recorded by Kalonji Changa in front of a live audience at the Boxcar Grocery in Atlanta June 2, 2013. It has been edited for clarity and flow.

is the way it is right now. The first question I want to ask is who is Assata Shakur, and when's the first time you made contact with her?

DHORUBA: First of all, let me say that it's a pleasure and an honor to be here with y'all, Black folks who have some consciousness, who can take time out on a Sunday to come and try to update and upgrade their information about relevant things. I feel very honored to have been able to be invited to this and come over and talk to you and listen to your questions.

Now, I know a lot of you are very young, few exceptions. To fully appreciate who Assata was, we have to try to understand the time that she lived in. We have to be conscious of where, when, and how, the environment, how things occurred and when they occurred, because history changes.

In the late '70s, Assata Shakur was—probably like most of you sisters here now—attending school at City College. At the time. there was a great upheaval of Black consciousness and City College was a hotbed of Black militancy. Professor Jeffries was teaching. Professor Small was up on the campus. We had Yosef ben-Jochannan doing lectures. You could see what type of environment it was, right? These are all these great historians that you've read about. There was a lot of kicking up at City College then. Imagine that being your history class and you are constantly involved in these different struggles that were going on. This was the environment that Assata was in during school. She lived right across the street up in the Harlem Heights from City College.

She was majoring or trying to go into the medical profession, so her majors were in that area. Of course she got interested in the Black Panther Party, and a couple of occasions we went up to City College to talk to students, just like I'm sitting here talking to you. She was motivated enough to come down to the Harlem office on Seventh Avenue to check out the party. She rode down with her little white hot pants on and a halter top and a little big-old poof Afro on the little bicycle. Rode all the way down to Harlem, parked in front of the office.

As everyone knows, Assata is a good-looking sister, so that caused a little scurry with the brothers in the office. The sister came to the office and she got involved with the community political education classes. We were having classes every week. She started coming to classes and started volunteering to do work, and then we formed a chapter, a National Committee to Combat Fascism (NCCF) chapter up in Washington Heights where she lived. She became part of that chapter with Isla Mason, Irving Mason, Frank Fields—who was later killed by the FBI terrorist task force in Florida—Twymon Myers—who was killed by the FBI task force in the South Bronx—and Anthony White who was killed by the FBI task force in Brooklyn. All of these folks were in her NCCF chapter. She became part of the medical cadres of the NCCF and the Black Panther Party that dealt with our free health programs.

We had free health programs in the community where we would set up a clinic and people would come in for sickle cell testing, or we would try to get volunteers from the hospitals, mainly conscious Black doctors who volunteered to come into the community and do free diagnostics, do free referrals, to do minimal invasive treatments and stuff like this. Assata got involved in that end of the party. That's how she got involved as a medical cadre. Unfortunately, this was right on the cusp of the split in the Black Panther Party.

COINTELPRO had worked so hard to divide the East Coast from the West Coast of the Black Panther Party, that it was becoming apparent that there were these tensions between the New York chapter on the East Coast region and the Central Committee on the West Coast. Myself and some other brothers and sisters increasingly turned towards our own cadres that we had been training and developing. Assata was one of them, and she became part and parcel of the infrastructure of the Black Liberation Army as the split developed.

She was a medical cadre in the Black Liberation Army. That's how she started out. She was running medical safe houses. In other words, we had access to hospital staff after hours. In New York and most places, if there's a bullet wound, you have to report it to the police. As soon as you go in the emergency, they'll call the police because they have a bullet wound. Of course, BLA members were getting wounded and they weren't getting wounded in car accidents, they were getting bullet wounds. One of the ways we would treat them is in the underground clinics we had, with all of the necessary first-aid stuff to be able to remove bullets. But if there was really serious stuff, we would have to get them into a hospital.

That's where Assata came in, because we had excellent contacts with doctors in Harlem Hospital, in Montefiore Hospital, in Lincoln Hospital, so we could bring in a person with a bullet wound through the back door, get him treated, and take him out without ever getting reported. This is what Assata's cell did at that time, and a number of brothers owe their lives to her. You may not know them. Some of them have passed away and some of them are still alive. That's what Assata's role was.

Basically, Assata became a revolutionary before she became a Black feminist. We have a lot of Black feminists now who see their support for Assata Shakur primarily as a persecuted woman by this big, bad bully of the United States government, ignoring the fact that Assata is being oppressed and repressed as a revolutionary, first and foremost. It is as a revolutionary Pan-African woman that she stands for the liberation and the emancipation of women, and Black women in particular. Assata was one of the better shooters in the Black Panther Party. Women tend to be better shooters than men. Don't ask me why, but they do. Once they get the training, there's something that kicks in. This type of training that we were able to give Assata added to her compassionate feeling for saving lives, for being involved on that level. I hope you follow what I'm saying. We were at war, and the enemy was trying to kill us.

One day, Assata was pulled over on the New Jersey Turnpike by the racist New Jersey State Troopers—and back then, driving down on the 95, on the Turnpike, you will get stopped as a Black person, driving while Black was usual, but more extreme back then. The New Jersey State Troopers had a reputation for this. We all know that. When Zayd, Sundiata, and Assata were stopped on the New Jersey Turnpike, you got to understand that they were at war. What would you think if the New Jersey State Troopers pulled you over, calling for backup, and he gets out of the car? What do you think happened when they stepped out of the car, with three Black folks and a person that looks like the most wanted woman in the Northeast, Assata Shakur, whom they even blamed for every armed robbery, every assault on policemen that occurred in the whole region, like she could be three places at one time? This is how fantastic it got. What would you do if a state trooper pulled you over and called for backup, and you stepped out of the car and you were wanted in forty-eight states? What would you do? All this guilt and innocence, "she had her hands up and she was shot." All of that may be true or not, but the fact of the matter is that we were at war. If the police got shot in the confrontation, that is to be expected.

Therefore, our support for Assata is not based on her guilt or innocence. It's based on our support for our right to self-defense, our right to national liberation, our right to self-determination, and our right to resist racist attacks. That's what the support for Assata and for all of the political prisoners really, really means.

You don't support them individually. You support the movement of which they became a part of and what they stand for, so guilt or innocence is irrelevant. I feel sorry for the families of the dead cops and all of that stuff, but we've got families, too. We suffered, too. There has been no reconciliation and no retribution on those who violated our rights and murdered us in cold blood.

I just want to say that when you think of Assata, and you think of what happened in that New Jersey Turnpike, don't think in terms of her being a victim. She was a revolutionary. A revolutionary is never a victim. Victims are people who don't make conscious decisions, who are victimized by a system and taken advantage of. A revolutionary is one who takes on the challenges of power, takes on the challenges of disempowerment, and tries to change the system. The system then deals out the injustice and the repression that is supposed to deal out to those who oppose it. She's no victim. There's no Scottsboro-Boys mentality here. None of those political prisoners in jail are in jail by coincidence. They're in jail by choice. I just wanted to put that out there as who Assata is and what she really stands for.

KALONJI: Cool. What I would like you to touch on—because I think that oftentimes we take for granted that folks understand what's what—is COINTELPRO. As you know, you see a lot of folks online throw the word around for anything. They truly don't understand what it is they're saying and what it is they're talking about. Can you give us a brief touch on what COINTELPRO is, and from COINTELPRO, maybe going to NEWKILL and CHESROB as well?

DHORUBA: OK. Assata was never a COINTELPRO target. I just told you how and when she joined the Black Panther Party. The COINTELPRO targets are in the documents of the FBI. She developed a file, as everybody did. Like anybody in this room, for instance, if I came and spoke to you and there was an FBI informant in this room and you raised your hand, I say, "Excuse me, sister, what's your name?" and you say, "My name is Monifa." They would open the file on Monifa and the FBI give you a number and everything. It'd be just Monifa, phonetic, Monifa. Then they'll try to find out who Monifa actually is. What's her real name? You follow what I'm saying?

Assata got into the files that way, but she was never a target. A target is someone who's identified and put in the Black Nationalist photo album, who's listed on the agitated index, and is also listed in FBI files as a major leader or a person that should be neutralized. That's the target of the counterintelligence program.

Now, the counterintelligence program, as we all may understand it has been taken out of context. People use it as generic term for repression of the Black movement. In some sense, that's sensible, but it's not true completely. It's not accurate. At the height of the counterintelligence program against the Black community between 1966 and its discovery in '71, 85 percent of all of the COINTELPRO operations aimed at the Black community were aimed at the Black Panther Party. In addition, Martin Luther King and the SCLC were targeted. All of these major organizations were targets to the counterintelligence program.

COINTELPRO stands for counterintelligence program. It was first initiated under that acronym against the Communist Party USA. The Communist Party USA was a longstanding organization we may be familiar with from reading DuBois, from reading Marcus Garvey, from reading Paul Robeson, who are all members—not Marcus, but Robeson and DuBois and Padmore, they were all members at one time or another. It was a very progressive organization, but it was linked to the Communist Party in Moscow. It followed the mass line and the dictates of the Revolutionary Party in Moscow, which was a Eurocentric revolutionary process that occurred at the end of the First World War.

Now, I don't want to go into a big, old history class about the war we were at the end of World War I and why Marcus Garvey was talking about Africa and imperialism. All of this is happening as I'm talking to you about the initiation of COINTELPRO, so keep that in the back of your mind.

At this particular time, the CPUSA in America was considered a threat by the US government because it was considered an agent of the Soviet Union. During World War II, this wasn't much of a problem because the Soviet Union was on the side of the United States against the Nazis and against Japan. It wasn't much of a problem. At the end of the war, with the US dropping an atom bomb on Japan, the Communist Party then became a hotbed of spies. We know about McCarthyism and about Paul Robeson. We know about Jackie Robinson denouncing Martin Luther King. We know about all of this. This is the Communist Party USA. It was led by a white man and a Black man who looked white.

Now, don't get me wrong. The CPUSA supported workers in this country. They helped build the unions in this country. They helped fight for the forty-hour week that we know in this country. They were the major advocates of the Scottsboro Boys, who brought attention to them internationally. They fought against the racist segregation in the South. The CPUSA was a progressive organization. I want you to understand this because what I'm about to say may paint them into a different light. They were a progressive organization, but they suffered from some of the residual effects of white supremacy and white-skin privilege and racism, and they were dominated by Zionists. Now, we need to understand that this is the Communist Party USA. This is why DuBois, who used to be the editor of their newspaper, fell out with them.

Here comes the CPUSA in the '60s. Black folks are burning down the place. Every summer, there's a hundred-and-something riots in the urban areas. The US is involved in a war with Vietnam that it's losing. It's drawing international anti-war sentiments around the world. People are demonstrating against US imperialism in Europe, in Asia, around the world. The CPUSA is in the forefront of this opposition to US imperialism. They're supporting the communists in Moscow, are supporting FRELIMO in Africa. They're supporting the PAIGC of Amilcar Cabral. They're supporting the liberation struggles in the Congo. They're on the right side of history in terms of supporting liberation movements in Africa, but here in America, they dissolve the issue of race and class. To them, in America, race is just a device and an instrument of the ruling class to divide the working class, and that therefore, we as Black people have to subsume our reality to that of the overall working class and fight for working-class unity of working-class rights.

People like myself, at that time, took exception to this. We said, "We didn't come here as workers. We came here as slaves, as tools of production, as tools of agrarian production. We've evolved since then into an independent sovereign people, scattered into a unique system of domestic colonialism." We had a right to self-determination. CPUSA disagreed with that analysis.

In the '60s, organizations like the RNA and the Black Panther Party, who advocated self-determination and advocated Black rights and Black independence, were marginalized and denigrated by the Communist Party, but they were colonized in the Black community. You see, the Black Panther Party had the overwhelming support of Black people in the community. They sympathized with the Black Panther Party. They may not have joined it, but when asked a question by the major networks, "What do you think about the Panthers?" They thought that they were brave young men who were standing up.

In a national poll, over 67 percent of Black people supported the Black Panther Party, and this could not stand. That's when the paradigm of emphasis on the Black Panther Party shifted. That's when the undercover agents and the reactionaries like Ron Karenga and these other pieces of doo-doo up in Chicago and all of these knuckleheads that you now think are great professors and stuff, that's when they trotted these Negroes out to talk about how the Black Panther Party was controlled by white folks. To this day, you have people like Judson Jeffries, if you get him on the side, he'll tell you that the downfall of the Black Panther Party was white women. They were haters then. They were going through school with dashikis and Afros trying to duck what was happening in the street based on Black-centric narrow nationalism. They weren't going to bust a grape with a ball-peen hammer in a fruit fight. These are the same guys. Now they're professors of departments, that's one of the reasons I don't get invited to colleges. They're heads of departments right now. I could name them, and you would say, "Really?" They're all over. You go to their lectures and they're brilliant lecturers. They lecture on Egyptology; they lecture on Black people's presence around the world. You know who I'm talking about? Because you know who do these lectures. I respect their knowledge. Don't get this twisted here. I respect knowledge, but I don't respect reactionary politics. There's a difference, you see.

Anyway, so my point is, here comes the Black movement, which is moving towards Black power, which is talking about how Black workers have their own historical impetus and that we have to reestablish our historical personality; that we have a relationship as workers to the colonizer in a system of colonial violence, not simply a relationship of class to class. You've got to remember; the Black Panther Party was the first national organization of Black men and women to come along that had a class analysis that was Marxist or Maoist in its viewpoints. You've got to understand what that meant to pork-chop nationalists like Ron Karenga and the cultural nationalists. They flipped on that era. They dismissed class struggle as just following a white man with a beard; this is what they would flip on. But we understood the limitations of Black faces in high places, they never did.

My brother Amiri Baraka whom I love dearly, who's my close comrade today and I'm honored to have lived in his time, because he's one of the best literary minds and writers in our time.[2] Back then, homeboy was on the wrong side of the paradigm. He was talking that wick-whack stuff about Black faces in high places. Ask about the Black mayor that betrayed them and look at Newark today. We got Black faces in high places all over the place and less power than we ever had. The Black Panther Party was right, and these Negroes were wrong.

That's one of the reasons why you don't hear about the Black Panther Party, except when they trot us out to vilify us. You have an Alice Walker who was tutored by Gloria Steinem—a CIA agent—who has this Black-male-hating form of Black feminism who writes an op-ed piece about the Black Panthers and the police being on a macho trip. We would just flip sides of the same coin, and we were just macho posturing. This is what this crazy woman said, Alice Walker. Then she turns around and says, "Support Assata Shakur because I met her when I was on a writer's conference in Cuba and I was touched by her spirit and her Blackness and all of this.

"Then I came back and she told me her version of what happened, and I believe Assata, that she was innocent and blah, blah, blah." This is Alice Walker. Alice Walker met Assata in exile in Cuba. She don't know jack shit about Assata with her good writing ass! People hold on to her words because she's an internationally renowned writer, which brings me to a next issue. The CPUSA, because they couldn't capture the Black militant movement created their own fronts.

---

2 Amiri Baraka was a writer of fiction, poetry, essays and other literary criticism, and cofounder of the Black Arts Movement in the 1960s. He died on January 9, 2014.

One of the fronts that they created was the Che-Lumumba Club in California. It was a book club, a reading club of Black students, mostly Marxists, on UCLA and USC campus who were students of Herbert Marcuse, a brilliant Marxist writer who taught at UCSD. He was brilliant, but he was Angela Davis' tutor in Marxism and she was a member of the Communist Party USA. She was a member of the Che-Lumumba Club, which was a Black front trying to center off Black militancy.

Around that time, George Jackson, who was a field marshal in the Black Panther Party, was in San Quentin prison and accused of murdering a prison guard.[3] This became the Soledad Brothers case, which soon began to grow in political significance, with the Black Panther Party as one of the major advocates and supporters of the Soledad Brothers. Angela came in contact with the defense committee of the Soledad Brothers, and she got involved from her position as a member of the Che-Lumumba Club.

The reason why I'm telling you this is very important because the Che-Lumumba was a foot of the CPUSA. The issue here were political prisoners who supposedly killed the prison guard, who were political and tied to the Black underground and the Black Panther Party. Angela Davis got involved with that front of the movement through her efforts to save George Jackson and the Soledad Brothers. That's how she got to the militant side of the movement. She got very close to Jonathan; she legally bought weapons for the Brothers. There was nothing illegal or clandestine about them, but they were in her name. When these weapons turned up into Marin County Court shootout in which a judge was killed, and several Black inmates who were comrades of George Jackson were killed, and Ruchell Magee and some others were captured alive, she was declared a fugitive and went underground.

The CPUSA gave her a handler who was an FBI informant while she was underground. That's how she got busted right here in New York, in the hotel. She went on trial and it became an international cause because the Communist Party USA put up Angela Davis as the face of Black America and Black militancy around the world. Wherever there was a Communist Party, there was a Free Angela defense committee. From Thailand to Azerbaijan there were

---

3 See *Soledad Brother: The Prison Letters of George Jackson* (New York: Lawrence Hill Books, 1994) and *Blood in My Eye* (New York: Random House, 1972).

free Angela Davis defense committees. She became the face of Black militancy to a lot of leftists in Europe.

Meanwhile, she's going on trial for conspiracy to commit murder, to kill this judge with Ruchell Magee, a prisoner and a comrade of George Jackson, who's been in prison almost his whole adult life. He was a soldier in jail who took the position that as a Black man and a slave in America, he had a right to try to escape. Of course, Angela's defense committee and all of them looked at him like he was crazy. Angela Davis had a Black attorney who was appointed to her by the CPUSA. Ruchell Magee represented himself with his right-of-a-slave-to-escape defense.

They separated the cases. Angela won her case, became a cause célèbre, toured the world to go to all those communist countries and tell them, "Thank you for your support." When she came back to the US, she held a press conference, along with Charlene Mitchell and others, and established the National Alliance to Combat Racist and Political Repression, which became another Communist Party front. This was supposed to deal with political prisoners. The first case they dealt with was Ben Chavis and the Wilmington case, and a little-known case of a sister who killed a prison guard in the South called Joan Little. She had killed a prison guard who had tried to rape her. They tried to paint her into a murderer and give her the chair. The National Alliance Against Racist and Political Repression took those two cases on.

Because the Communist Party did not believe in Black folks' right to self-determination and to self-defense, and they had this rule about racism, they refused to support any Black Panther Party cases that were involved with the shooting of policemen or that was involved with the armed front of the Black Liberation Movement. This dichotomy, this division started by these leftist movements defined how we looked at political prisoners for the next twenty years. You want to know why there are political prisoners in jail today? Why you don't know nothing about it? This is where it started.

KALONJI: Knowing what you're talking about with Angela and the whole Communist Party, why is it that most people associate Angela Davis with the Black Panther Party?

DHORUBA: Again, it's a misconception. Angela Davis was never a member of the Black Panther Party. She became a target of COINTELPRO as a result of her work in the Che-Lumumba Club and being a member of the Communist Party, but we know that by 1968, '69 and '70, that the major focus of COINTELPRO wasn't on the Communist Party, it was on the Black Liberation Movement. It was on Dr. King. It was on the Black Panther Party. It was on Fred Hampton in Chicago. It was on the Panther 21 in New York. It's not that she wasn't a COINTELPRO target, she may well have been, but it was not under the rubric of being a leading Black militant, but as being a member of the Communist Party USA.

The COINTELPRO initially started with the CPUSA. They were heavily infiltrated for decades. They were more infiltrated than the Nation of Islam, which the police, by the time of Malcolm, feared more than the CPUSA. Angela was never a member of the Black Panther Party. She became involved, as I pointed out, with the defense committee for the Soledad Brothers, as a member of the Che-Lumumba Club. The Black Panther Party supplied all of the soldiers, all of the footwork, all of the wherewithal for that defense committee of the Black Panther Party on the West Coast in support of George and his defense committee, wholeheartedly, to the point of trying to break him out of jail.

KALONJI: When you talk about counterinsurgency, a few words that people don't hear about are NEWKILL and CHESROB. Can you break down what NEWKILL and CHESROB are, since we denounced the whole COINTELPRO notion in regards to Assata's case?

DHORUBA: I believe it was early 1971 when some white radicals broke into the FBI office in Media, Pennsylvania. I was in the box in Comstock in '71. I started twenty-five to life. I had just got convicted for the shooting of two cops in New York, their wounding and everything, and I was in the box. Then I read about this COINTELPRO. The kids that broke into the office released all the information to the media. For the first time people hearing about this secret FBI program called COINTELPRO, which was targeting Black leaders and radicals in this country for neutralization, for defamation, and all of these things.

When I heard this, I called up one of my attorneys, Robert Bloom, who was one of the leading attorneys on the Panther 21 case, and I said, "I believe that I have a COINTELPRO file." I know I didn't do what they said I did, Even though I'd happen to agree with the fact that it was done, it wasn't me. I said, "Let's see how they worked this frame-up." I know they had information that it hadn't been me. They had all the information, but they just didn't give it up, so I decided to file a suit. Then, of course, the feds said, "We don't have nothing but his criminal record." They gave me about ten or eleven volumes of a thousand pages each of my criminal record. My criminal conviction, the 21 case, everything that everybody knew about.

I happened to have one of the first Black female judges that were appointed to the federal court—I think she was appointed by LBJ—and that was Mary Johnson Lowe, may Allah be pleased with her. She was an old civil rights sister from the NAACP Civil Rights Defense Fund. Came up with Thurgood and all of them, and she was now a federal judge. She sat in the Southern District, and that's where my case went. Of course, the FBI continued lying over the months, saying, "We don't have nothing on him. We gave him everything."

Then, it just so happens that the attorney in the Fred Hampton case in Chicago, who was trying to sue the Chicago police and the FBI for the murder of Fred Hampton, were also very close associates and friends with my attorneys. In fact, they all started out in the same law commune in New York around the Panther 21 case. They said that they'd got some files there with my name on it—some of the COINTELPRO files in Chicago—and Bloom said, "Oh, yeah, well, send them down." They sent down about 15–20 pages with my name on it. My lawyer then turned to the judge and said, "Judge Lowe, these are FBI documents with the acronym COINTELPRO on them, and they got my client's name on it, and we never seen them before. They said they gave us everything."

Girlfriend went off. She says, "Y'all have lied to me all these months." She said, "I'm going to tell you something. All of you, all the federal defenders, the Justice Department,"—she started naming them—"All of you, every file that you have now on the Black Panther Party, on the New York chapter of the Black Panther party, on all the chapters of the Black Panther Party, on this man and on his family, and on his associates, will be delivered into this court and turned over to the plaintiff."

I stayed in the Federal House of Detention for a year, almost fifteen months, reading files. Every week, they would bring in twenty, thirty volumes. I got the Chicago chapter files, I got the New York files, I got the Boston files, I got them all, and here comes CHESROB and NEWKILL. Once counterintelligence program was discovered and revealed publicly, they changed the name. They changed the game. They said in their memo that, "We can no longer support conspiracy cases." That, "We have to go after particular criminal charges against these people and get them convicted on these criminal charges and forget this conspiracy case because every conspiracy case we had, we lost."

They lost the 21 case. They lost the Chicago 7 case. They lost the conspiracy with the LA and the RNA case. They lost all these cases. They were all conspiracy cases. Now they were coming with the hard stuff, criminal prosecutions, "Let's form a task force," they thought, because these people were criminals and they were terrorists, so they formed a joint terrorist task force. The joint anti-terrorist task force, which was comprised of the NYPD, the New York State Troopers, the FBI, and they operated out of Giuliani's office in the Southern District. They went specifically after ex-Black Panthers and after members that they considered targets. The FBI started sharing all of this information to them about who we were, where we were, what we were all about.

A couple of days after I was acquitted in absentia in the 21 case, two cops were killed up in Washington Heights in Assata's neighborhood. The Attorney General and the head of the FBI then went to Nixon's White House and had a secret meeting with him. Back then, Nixon was recording everything, remember. This is the Watergate period. J. Edgar Hoover, the director of the FBI, is there talking about, "We have these cop killings that's going on in New York and they seem to be spreading everywhere. We have two more cops who were killed in Atlanta. We had another cop that was ambushed and killed in the police station in San Francisco, and one more in LA. It looks like there's a Black underground in this country that's targeting policemen and we got to do something about this." Nixon made it a priority for the Justice Department to find these individuals and apprehend and neutralize them. This new initiative came out of the White House was called NEWKILL, "new killing of police officers." It targeted all of the former members of the 21, all of the Black Panther Party political prisoners, all of those who went underground. Assata also became a target of the FBI under NEWKILL, because she was in the medical cadre of the BLA.

At this point, I had already been busted, but there were a number of BLA cells operating in the country and in prison and we had formed ourselves into a communications network. This became a command-and-control structure for those brothers and sisters who were ripping and running on the outside who were more or less independent and more or less divorced from each other in terms of coordination. This was the period in which some of you may have read this document called "Message to the Black Movement: A Political Statement from the Black Underground." This message from the Black underground was written from prison by political prisoners on behalf of the brothers of the armed front of the underground who were still out in the open, out in the streets.

There was this period when the so-called Black activists began to betray those brothers and sisters who had taken up arms against the enemy. This is when the preachers started talking about, "This anti-police violence wasn't no good." This is when the police department started hiring public relations specialists and started initiating block watches and these different programs and snitch programs in the community. Of course, this marked the rise of the people that we know today, the Al Sharptons and the talk show hosts that you have on talk show radio today, the O'Reilly's and all of these knuckleheads.

This is how they got their play. At this time after they finished with COINTELPRO and they realized they could no longer pursue us on that level, they established this anti-terrorist program, this anti-urban guerrilla program, and then they became aware of Assata and these armed robberies, which was one of the major ways the Black Liberation Army raised funds. The way we went about doing it, is that we identified sources of capital, like banks, armored cars, and drug dealers—specifically heroin dealers. It was this campaign that provided the funding. It was under this campaign that Assata became so notorious, because any place there was a Black woman with an Afro that did a robbery, it was Assata. The sister actually sat down and read two different accounts, herself, where she was in three different places at the same time. They tried doing special articles. They had a mugshot of her. Go look at the old newspaper clippings. You can see what I'm saying. They had this old mugshot of Assata with her face all styled up she looked like Harriet Tubman. You know how they photographed Black folks when they arrest you and rough you up, your hair is all on, and it mashed down. Your lips all swelled up on one side and they take a picture of you. Then they put that up in the newspaper.

Now, ain't nobody going to recognize Assata compared to this picture because Assata is a good-looking woman. She could walk right before you. You'd be looking at the picture and say, "Man, you know, they after your sister." Their thing backfired on them. Anyway, they had her as the queen bee, as the mother hen, they called her, who kept everybody's guns oiled, kept them in discipline, tucked them in at night, made sure that they had everything they had needed when they went out to rob a bank. This was Assata. She was a revolutionary mammy. She kept the babies safe and running. This is how they had her. Go look at the propaganda.

She became the number one target. They established a whole program called CHESROB, "Chesimard armed robberies." Both the CHESROB and NEWKILL operations were authorized out of the Nixon White House. Of course, the tapes of that meeting disappeared. The only recollections we have stem from the Church Committee, where the testimony of Justice Department officials who were present at the meeting indicated that this is what happened. But the actual tape, the recordings of what was said, who was identified, disappeared. How did ours disappear, and theirs didn't? This was something the Church Committee never got into. How did the FBI interface with local law enforcement to kill and repress Black militants? This has never been investigated. The Church Committee stopped short of it, and this is where we're at now. We have to get Black-elected officials, the Congressional Black Caucus, to reopen up these investigations as to how organized police power infected and affected law enforcement's relationship to Black activists and Black political leaders.

It's on the local level that we've been co-opted and disrupted. It's on the local level that we've been misrepresented. It's on the local level that we got these Negro politicians that you have here in Atlanta and these jive-ass Black sheriffs talking about they're going to keep the streets clean. They sound just like the crackers. "We running the plantation now and we are both the plantation master and the slaves." Yeah. Look at the po-po. Things have gotten this way because of this history. This is only a small part of this history that I'm talking about, the stuff that we were directly involved in. There's stuff that was happening internationally in which we were indirectly involved in, like the case of Sekou Odinga.

If Sekou Odinga was a white boy, they would get Brad Pitt to play his role as a *Bourne Supremacy*-type character. Here's a man, Sekou Odinga, who was one of the Panther 21. When the SWAT teams came to get us at four o'clock in the morning, he heard them organizing down in the street and escaped. He slid down the drainpipe, from four stories up. He slipped out behind the police, who had cordoned off the whole neighborhood, escaped down South, hijacked a plane, and went to Cuba. Odinga stayed in Cuba with Eldridge Cleaver before moving on to Algeria as part of the international section. He later worked with the Palestinians, and the PLO, George Habash, and the PFLP, then went and trained in the Congo.

Then, when the Black Panther Party chapter in Algeria dispersed, he went to North Korea, trained with FRELIMO, came back into the United States through Canada, and landed in the Black underground and has helped Assata escape from prison. He was the mastermind of that. If that don't sound like a Hollywood script, I don't know what does. [They laugh.] Sekou Odinga.

KALONJI: Coming back to Assata, why do they feel that she is a threat now with this whole $2 million bounty? Also, we just heard that Ben Jealous, the president and tap dancer for the NAACP, stated that they haven't taken a position. Why hasn't Ben Jealous and folks like Reverend Al taken a position on the Assata Shakur case?

DHORUBA: I don't know if we respect the position Reverend Al takes, given his history with trying to entrap Shakur, but I think we need to understand why this has been done.[4] She hasn't had no articles in the newspaper. We haven't been reading her speeches anymore. She hasn't been exhorting Black folks to rebellion. She's quietly in exile in Cuba. Then all of a sudden, boom, they hold

4 Al Sharpton, who was working as a federal informant at the time, allegedly tried to set up a meeting with Assata Shakur in 1983.

press conference to claim that Assata has been added to the top ten terrorists wanted by the FBI. Everybody's like, "Whoa."

Everybody comes out and says it's just about persecution of a Black woman and blah, blah, blah. The fact of the matter is that we have to look at what's happening right now with the Obama Administration geopolitically. What is Obama's new policy in Latin America? Just two weeks before Obama did this, a couple of weeks before he did this, he met with the new Mexican president. He announced America's new emphasis in Latin America on support of economic assistance and a de-emphasis on the war on drugs and on military assistance to the region. This is because of the success of individuals like Chavez, Lula's recent regime in Brazil, and the brother in Peru, Morales; these forces have shifted the geopolitical power in Latin America to the left. Of course, Cuba has always been there. Cuba's always been a stalwart of not just Africa, but of progressive movements in Latin America.

Chavez was a threat to the US. He was a younger version of Fidel as far as they were concerned. That's why he might have been killed, as some suspect. It's funny that all of these leaders die of cancer before the age of fifty, you see. Anyway, this paradigm of leftist progressive governments has shattered the whole US hegemony in the region.

The Justice Department is run by Obama. That's his Justice Department. He appointed to oversee it. We are not going to put anyone on an international terrorist list, on the most-wanted list, even if it's symbolic without the OK of the White House. Obama signed off on Assata doing this. Why would he do that? He could still pursue his policy without never mentioning her. It's because of the police, who keep trying to lock her in jail, and who said she's a cop killer. If there's any type of reconciliation in Cuba, any change in the status of Cuba and the US, they have to give her up. They can't let a person who killed policemen live in freedom in exile because it's their position that anybody who kills a cop should never get out of jail. Period. That's why the political prisoners are still in jail. They're not in jail for no other reason than they're charged with killing cops.

We're only going to be free when we break the political power of the police over the state and federal political infrastructure. It's simple. Writing letters, demonstrating in the streets is not going to get them out of jail. It's removing the political power of the police.

We've got Black leaders talking about reform, sensitivity training. "We need more of this. We need more of that." Nah, we need less cops and more community control of public safety. When we look at this issue around how Assata got mentioned is because of the political power of the law enforcement. Obama needs the political backing of law enforcement in America. He can't proceed without it. He signs off on their right, on their plea, on their political move to make sure that any type of reconciliation that goes down with Cuba, she's in the mix.

Now, me, personally, I'd give the Cubans notice, "If y'all give up Assata, you betrayed your own revolution. That's the end of your revolution." That's the end of the Cuban Revolution.

The Cuban Revolution has been one of the most significant events for Africans and people of African ancestry in the twentieth century. It were the Cubans who unconditionally supported the liberation movements in Africa; who sent soldiers; who sent doctors; who died in the Congo, in Cuito Cuanavale. It were the Cubans who helped free our people on the African continent. Without Fidel Castro, they would've never done that.

To me, the Cuban Revolution has always been something that we should support. It's the Cubans who protect Assata Shakur when nobody else will. If they give her up, that's the end of their revolution. That's the end of their principles. That's how we need to look at it. We need to understand what their contribution and their sacrifice has been. They've been pressured to do this for a long time and they have never done it. They should be praised for that.

The US knows the importance of keeping this police assignment. What do they do? They send your homeboy down to Cuba to let them know what the real deal is. They send Jay-Z and Beyoncé. They take a vacation in a country that's blockaded. They're on the beach, chilling. "Y'all, Barack, you need to be down here with Michelle kicking it on the beach with me. I just flew down on my private jet and we chilling." How are you going on vacation in a country that's blockaded and it's illegal for US citizens to travel to? There are only four conditions you could travel to Cuba and none of them is as a tourist: as a journalist, for religious reasons, for medical reasons, and on a special permit, for family reasons. There's protocol now that if you have family in Cuba, you can travel back and forth. He had to get a special visa from the State Department to travel to Cuba. His homeboy is Barack. He always talks about how him and Barack are on a first-name basis. See, the State Department belongs to Barack. Barack's State Department gave him a visa, and the Cubans accepted it. Now, the Cubans don't know Jay-Z from a hole in the wall. All they know is that they listen to his music and what they see about Jay-Z. What do Cubans know about Jay-Z except that he's an entertainer, a billionaire, well-known around the world, that he's married to one of the most beautiful women in the world, and that he's cronies with Barack Obama? That's all they know about.

All I'm saying is, he gets a visa, takes his entourage down and he's chilling on the beach. What is involved in traveling to a foreign country when you don't have a visa? Who's on the entourage? You know that this was a special visa. This was a special occasion, and the Cubans assigned a special liaison to handle him and his whole trip while he was in Cuba. I know how it goes. This liaison is going to report back to the Central Committee and to his superiors exactly what was transmitted to him about everything that's happening here. From the hotel staff telling you what sheet side they slept on, to everything else. Believe me, before they left, the Cuban Central Committee had a whole report on what they were about, why they were there, what they said, and when they said it. It's a better foil to send a message to the Cubans but through a Negro like this. Who handled this protocol?

Nobody ever asked these guys this. "Jay-Z, did you in fact provide cover for an attempt to communicate with the Cuban government about Assata Shakur? Yes or no, did you?" Because you got to remember, he may not have been even been aware of it. It might have been the person that's making his arrangements as a State Department agent. State Department said, "This is very delicate, Mr. Jay-Z. We have to accompany you on this trip." Look what happened in China with Nixon, who opened up relations with China with ping pong. There was a ping-pong team that played in the international tournament that was scheduled to play in Beijing. The US had no relationship with China. In fact, the UN representative from China came from the island of Taiwan at the time. Now, here's an island with twelve million people that's representing 1.5 billion in the UN. They had to deal with the fact that China was becoming a superpower. Well, there was an opportunity. There's a ping-pong tournament, and the US ping-pong team was in the semifinals. They sent a US State Department handler along with the ping-pong team. The handler interfaced secretly with the Chinese government and said, "Richard Nixon is interested in establishing normalizing relationships. This is what Henry Kissinger would want to do. We would do this and you would do that." That's what happened. As a result, Nixon was able to travel to China, get on the news, "It's opening up China to the US," and the rest is history. It was a ping-pong team that started it.

When we talk about the Cuban blockade coming down, sink back and remember that it was Jay-Z and Beyoncé who started it. Girlfriend was on the case. She was the Mata Hari of your time.

AUDIENCE MEMBER: As citizens, is there anything we can do to support our political prisoners, essentially get Assata off the list? I heard you say something about the police state, and about advocating for community control of public safety?

DHORUBA: One of the things that we can do is we can organize locally, by city, by community, to decentralize public safety and get it on a referendum, get in on the ballot. Now, the fact that we're trying to put it on referendum means we have to get out in the streets and raise votes. We have to agitate. We have to give people information about why they should vote for decentralization.

When we talk about public safety, we're not just talking about police. We're talking about fire. We're talking about emergency responses. We have the examples of Hurricanes Katrina and Sandy to show that we have to be more trained and more in tune as a community to be our own first responders. We're talking about closed firehouses, and the need to open them back up, and brothers and sisters need to be trained in public safety so they can volunteer in these firehouses. We have to talk about ambulance services, EMS, community health.

See, we bury these knuckleheads in public safety, not cops. We're talking about public safety districts and that the district boards should have public safety boards that we are at. They should determine the policies for public safety administration in their districts. Those districts that don't have resident clauses, like the financial district or where the office buildings are at, let that accrue to the state and to the city, because we know that nobody's living there. It's about property. It's about regulation of property and garbage collection. All this is public safety. Public health is public safety.

When we organize on that level, sister, all these questions come up: mass incarceration, the criminal justice system, why we're being marched through these courts, all the taxpayers' money that's being used for minuscule amounts of marijuana and DUI cases, hundreds of thousands of dollars they raising. All of these issues then become, "What are the cops doing? I didn't elect you to pass this bill." You've got to remember, everything they do to us, is because our elected officials passed a bill. We just didn't know anything about it.

Organizing, that means organizing political clubs. Organize a political club here in Atlanta, all y'all need it. Then you can have your little political congregations and you start giving out information into your little district, to your people.

Then, when a guy wants to run for the district, for your little district representative or your whatever, he has to come to your political club, and you say, "What's in it for us? Why should we vote for you?" "I think you should vote for me because such and such." "Well, we have this issue. Are you going to stand up for this issue for us, and then we'll vote for you?" Become an independent political action club. You're not with the Democrats, you're not with the Republicans, you are independent. Hold these knuckleheads to account. Mass incarceration occurred on the watch of these Negro leaders. They weren't absent, they were the ones calling for more cops. They were the ones talking about, "We need more prisons." They were the ones talking about all this smack about our youth being out of control. Now we got 1.6 million people in jail, nearly 40 percent of them Black folks, that subtracts almost 1.5 percent of the voting power of the Black community nationally.[5]

Now everybody's up and arms about Michelle Alexander's book, and this is, "The New Jim Crow. This is a terrible thing that happened." You Negroes let it happen.

AUDIENCE MEMBER: There seems to be a generational gap. Why do you think that is?

---

5 According to Prison Policy Initiative, as of 2024, the United States carceral system held over 1.9 million people in state and federal prisons, local jails, juvenile correctional facilities, immigration detention facilities, and Indian country jails, as well as in military prisons, civil commitment centers, state psychiatric hospitals, and prisons in the US territories. See Wendy Sawyer and Peter Wagner, *Mass Incarceration: The Whole Pie 2024*, March 14, 2024, https://www.prisonpolicy.org/reports/pie2024.html.

DHORUBA: Yes, there is a gap. That gap is intentional, because one of the purposes of the Counterintelligence Program—and it's stated in their documentation—is that we have to ensure that each generation of African youth don't become revolutionaries. That they understand that the only revolutionary is a dead revolutionary. That they would rather be a basketball player or sports figure, or artist respected by whites and Blacks alike, than to be a revolutionary. What that translates into, and this has been the same since slavery, is that each generation, especially of Black men, has to grow up alone. The only unifying glue that has provided continuity has been the Black family in certain basic Black institutions like the Black church, you see. They provided some framework of continuity, but each generation of Black males had to find out for themselves what it was all about, because the last generation was wiped out.

People had to rediscover Malcolm. Why did they have to rediscover him? Because there was no movement left. People are rediscovering Assata. If they didn't put Assata up on a Ten Most Wanted list, we wouldn't be having this conversation now. The enemy hasn't forgotten what we are and what we could be.

We've forgotten because they made sure that what he learns can't be passed on to you. You've got to understand that in the counterinsurgency manuals that were circulated in the '60s and '70s, a primary objective of counterinsurgency was to create the inability of the guerrillas to pass on leadership knowledge and skills to another generation of guerrillas. This is why they had to kill Amilcar Cabral. This is why Patrice Lumumba was killed. This is why Eduardo Mondlane was killed. This is why all of these freedom fighters were killed, so that they would not pass on what they have learned to another generation of freedom fighters.

This is why the Vietnamese succeeded, because they understood this and they made it clear that they didn't know that they were supposed to lose this battle. They didn't have no expectation to lose it because they were going to fight from one generation to the next. That's how they won. They were able to pass on the struggle from one generation to the next until the enemy tired and withdrew.

We have to fight and stand up for ourselves. Start to do political work in the community around local issues that change people's understanding of what their relationship to this institutional public safety is. I thought we was paying these guys taxes. They treat us like we're working for them. And it's not just about training; it's about the very institution of policing in America that is based on a different model, a different paradigm that's no longer applicable to the inner-city Black people.

The police chief and the office of police chief has to go. It's obsolete. You could have the best-trained police chief in the world and crime still goes up. You still have the same police brutality, and everybody starts calling for his resignation ten years, five years from now for the same thing. It's obvious it doesn't work. Just try something new. This is where we come in, getting the people to understand. Once we do that, then we can talk about changing how the parole board looks at a political prisoner that comes up in front of them. All they're saying to them is, when a political prisoner comes up for parole, "Well, we can't release you because it's the conditions of the crime. It's the circumstances of the crime." The circumstances of the crime are never going to change. It's in the past. You can't change that. Now here's a brother sitting in front of you with three degrees, a master's in this, he's a professor in that. He's been in jail for thirty-five years, and you're talking about he can't get parole because of the nature of the crime?

You look at Europe, and all of the revolutionaries or radicals who killed people, who killed police in Italy, the Red Brigades in Italy, they're all out of prison. The Red Army Faction, the Baader-Meinhof group in Germany, out of prison. The PFLP, or the people that ran with Carlos the Jackal, out of prison. Everybody's out of prison and been out of prison for the past ten, fifteen years. Our political prisoners are still in jail.

When they go to the parole board, what do we do? We write letters to the parole board saying that we want them out. What does the police do? They trot out the widow of the policeman that was killed, who by now is remarried, got hundreds of thousands of dollars in compensation, and her kids are grown up and she's got grandkids. They trot her out, "I'm still suffering from the death of my husband. He should never be let out of prison. He killed my husband." It's only the PBA, the policeman union that's bringing them out to do this because in the parole rules, the parole board's supposed to hear every side of the community's view. We come out and say, "Our community wants him." The police come out and say, "We don't want him out." Who raises power more? Theirs. If we had more political power than them, he'd be out.

KALONJI: I want to point out, too, why it's mandatory for us to continue to study. One of the things we do is we depend on other people's versions of our truth. We depend on whatever is posted on Facebook, whatever is on Wikipedia, whatever they say on the internet. What happens online is low-intensity warfare. Right now, when we talk about counterinsurgency and all that, they took it to another level. Instead of us looking for what's real, we'll look at who's producing what. You're going to get an Angela Davis in a full-on political prisoner movie, but it'd be the watered-down version. Again, Angela Davis's codefendant, Ruchell Magee has been locked up for over forty years. Assata Shakur's daughter's father is right here in Georgia. Kamau Sadiki, he's been locked up for the last ten years. Stephanie B. Manis, the judge here railroaded him and Imam Jamil, H. Rap Brown, right here in Atlanta. We got to be clear of what's going on, and we got to be able to understand what's what.

Part of the whole thing with this whole Assata forum as well, now that they put her on this terrorist list, is that we have to be careful what it is we're saying on social media, because you don't want to be viewed as supporting a so-called terrorist. We really got to take it to another level.

Another thing we have to do, too, is get in touch with the Congressional Black Caucus. Put some fire under their ass and ask them to speak on this case. Ask Al Sharpton why he's not speaking. Part of the reason why he's not talking is because he wore a wire in the '80s to try to entrap Assata Shakur. He talked about in his own book about wearing wires and working for the feds. We forget about that, because like Martin Luther King said, we've got an eight-day memory. We get all hyped about whatever the flavor of the month is.

One week it's Oscar Grant, Sean Bell, Troy Davis, Trayvon Martin, whoever's next, that's who we are. Now everybody's talking about Assata like it's a brand-new case when in reality we know that they put the million-dollar bounty on her in 2005. That was eight years ago. One of the best ways you can support Assata Shakur is by doing what she said. Supporting the other political prisoners, supporting her codefendants. You got folks like her codefendant Sundiata who has been locked up for over forty years.

DHORUBA: If you were to just write some people like, some of these knucklehead producers, these people that you all might respect, whether there's these multi-moguls that do movies like Ice Cube or whatever, and say, "How come you all never do a movie on a genuine militant Black hero?" They would say like, "Who are you talking about?" "Sekou Odinga." Do you all do any research on him? He don't know who you're talking about. When they do the research, they are like, "Whoa."

KALONJI: Ice Cube used to visit Imam Jamil right here in the West End, in the community. Ice Cube would come here whenever he was in Atlanta to go see H. Rap Brown (Imam Jamil al-Alamin). Once Imam Jamil al-Alamin caught that case, Ice Cube did like most of these other Negroes and act like he forgot.

DHORUBA: You see what happened with Common and Obama. Obama reaching out to the hip-hop generation and trying to be like he's hip and all of that. Common is a respected artist who has some politics and who has some conscience. He ain't a 2 Chain or Lil' Wayne. He's artistic, he's a good actor.

Now, Obama didn't really realize that Common had visited Cuba and hung out with Assata and is on tape talking about how honored he was to be in her presence. When he went to the White House, of course, the police have this tape [of Common's visit to Assata], they've seen it on YouTube. They said, "What! This is the dude that sympathized with the cop killer. He was down in Cuba with Assata Shakur." Now Obama had to backtrack.

Common wrote some stuff about how he didn't want to jeopardize this and backed out. Did you notice when Jay-Z wrote these articles about his recent trip, he had words in there to the effect—what were the words?—that communism is confusing, that his mic was made in China and all of this shit. Then Common came out and wrote a response to him, and then Farrakhan gets on TV talking about, "My brother Jay-Z. He did a power move, brother. You've already done it." Trying to get that Jay-Z money for the next Saviours' Day. We got to be careful, man. We confuse these anytime the state trots out Black leadership and these hip-hop artists, so on and so forth, it's all game. Whenever they bring these hip-hop artists to sponsor, cosponsor, whatever it is they're talking about, if you don't see these hip-hop artists in the community, then you could disregard that and treat it as entertainment.

When we did that interview about the Jay-Z-going-to-Cuba piece, Obama sending him down, so on and so forth, people didn't want to believe it, because, "Well, he's just a rapper." You can reach whoever you want to reach. If Common can reach Assata, Jay-Z can reach Assata.

The thing about President Obama is that he's a real slick dude. He's charismatic. He's charming, plays basketball, eats chicken, goes to burger joints, all of that. At the end of the day, he is a representative of white supremacy. He represents the forces that keep us down. Now, we being Black and in love with the thought of us making it, we look at him as a symbol of Black heroics or something. He has a Black wife and all of that. That's game. White folks knew that we wouldn't be trusting too many old white men much longer. Now, comes along this guy, whatever, and it's all good. When we're talking about Obama, we're not dissing him as a family man. We're not saying that it's not good to see a Black role model. At the same time, what's your politics? If your politics is to take us out, man. . . . This dude has sent more drones overseas and here in the States than George Bush. In thirty-five different countries, there are American soldiers training so-called antiterrorists, anti-Al-Qaeda forces. Over thirty people have been killed in northern Nigeria in one month alone by the Nigerian government who are operating on US drone intelligence and SEAL team advisors.

Ellen Sirleaf Johnson, the (now former) president of Liberia who supposedly represents the new face of African leadership, this new Black face of Black women leaders. She was in Washington, DC two weeks ago when her Minister of Security, the head of her internal security threatened the whole journalistic corps of Liberia, said, "If you write any counter-article, any negative article about us or about our government, I'm going to put you in jail. You got the pen. I got guns." Come to find out, her personal security person was in the US military for five years. He's a Liberian who served in the US military for five years. Now, he's in charge of her security. Who does he take his orders from?

The US has a policy of recruiting foreigners to serve in the US military. They sign a four, five-year contract. After that contract is up, they get citizenship. I've had friends from Ghana, Nigeria, and Liberia join the US military, served five years, and got their citizenship. What the US has done is they flipped that around. You know what kind of value that becomes. Whereas this guy was five years in the US military, he's now the chief security for the president of Liberia. He's so arrogant. There's nothing that's worse than an African with power who is ignorant and arrogant. There's nothing worse. Even an ignorant, arrogant white boy is not that bad. You've met your match when you meet that.

My point is that Obama represents the greatest deception of African people since the Emancipation Proclamation. Seriously. Historically, he does. Black folks are going to feel it in the next thirty-six months after he leaves office. Everything that he's done, we would have never allowed a cracker to do. We would have been up in arms talking about how these are the last days of the Black. We're going to be exterminated and all. We'd have been crazy by now if there was a white boy sitting in the White House. It's the same thing with the rest of the world.

You know that more people celebrated Obama getting elected internationally than we did. People were dancing in the streets in Paris. Africans were talking about us with the first African president and how everything was going to change. Even Muslims were like, "Oh, yeah. Cool. He's going to become a Muslim anyway, right? He got a name like Obama Hussein, whatever." Then, we knew what was going to happen. He got the Nobel Peace Prize and he ain't never did nothing. He was only in office for thirty days when he got the Nobel Peace Prize. We knew right then that he was going the same way as Mandela, he was going the same way as Anwar Sadat, all of whom got a Peace Prize in partnership with a piece of shit.

I ain't going to mince my words. I'm sorry. That's what they were. Henry Kissinger got a Nobel Peace Prize. They couldn't give it to him by himself. They had to hook him up with Le Duc Tho, the head negotiator of North Vietnam. Why? Because they negotiated a geopolitical watershed, the end of the Vietnam War. That was so important geopolitically to the West that they had to get a Peace Prize for it. De Klerk and Mandela; they couldn't give Mandela the prize by himself. That would have been saying too much. He was the leader of an armed underground. He was in prison. He led a liberation movement that was Black. They had to prove that once this power was transferred, white folks were still welcome in South Africa, and they didn't have to worry about power changing at all.

It didn't change. The ANC [African National Congress] that we thought was a liberation movement.

There were a bunch of lawyers who were forced into a liberation struggle and once they had the opportunity to legally become lawyers again, that's exactly what they did. All of them, all ANC cronies, they're all billionaires now, all consultants. 85 percent of the land that belonged to white folks that was taken from Africans still belongs to white folks and still is producing diamonds and the gold that Black folks don't control. That's why Mandela got a Peace Prize along with de Klerk, to make sure that South African experience worked.

Then we had the other one, Menachem Begin, who was a terrorist who led the Irgun, who blew up the King David Hotel and killed dozens of British citizens. Got a Peace Prize with Anwar Sadat. Why? Sadat was the only knucklehead to go and sign the peace treaty with Israel. That's what he did that ended the paradigm of power in the Middle East. Remember Andy Young was the ambassador to the United Nations? Jimmy Carter fired him because he had initiated a back-channel dialog with the Palestinians. He wasn't authorized to do so. There couldn't be no dialog with the Palestinians at that point. He was fired. At that particular point in time, the US government had decided that we understood that Andy Young had become a charter member of the Trilateral Commission. Remember about the Trilateral Commission and Carter? Remember all that stuff? Read the Trilateral Commission's Report on the Middle East, and what it said would be a solution to the problem in the Middle East. It said that Israel was surrounded by hostile Arab powers. The three primary powers were Syria, Egypt, and Jordan And one of these powers had to be knocked out of the equation because Israel could not fight another war on all those fronts. They had to remove one of these powers from the equation. Two of these powers were clients of the Soviet Union. They had to win over one of them from the Soviet Union.

They went after Egypt because of Abdel Nasser and the concept he had fostered of Pan-Arabism, of Arab unity. This wasn't anti-Black. This wasn't anti-sub-Saharan. It was anti-imperialist. You've got to remember that to the Arabs, the imperial powers weren't Africans, they were the Turks and Europeans. Anwar Sadat was convinced that he would get American military aid, support, maybe keep him in power if he would sign a peace treaty with Israel. He did, and his ass is dead.

They gave him a Nobel Peace Prize, so we know that the Nobel Peace Prize was always given to people at a certain point in time where it was important to pull the wool over everybody's eyes about how things had changed when in fact they didn't.

That's why Obama got a Peace Prize, and he's been at war since. Obama's been raging war ever since he became president. How does a war president get a Peace Prize? Did you read Obama's acceptance of his Peace Prize? He talked about "justifiable war." If Martin Luther King was alive, he'd have rolled over. Go read King's acceptance of the Nobel Peace Prize and then read Obama's. There was a man who's accepted the moral and ethical responsibility of being an international representative of peace, a symbolic representative of what a better world could be. Whereas Obama is talking about how sometimes we've got to take up arms against tyrants, and in his mind, that is people like Hitler, but he's going to trot him out to compare Black folks and Black people fighting for their liberation.

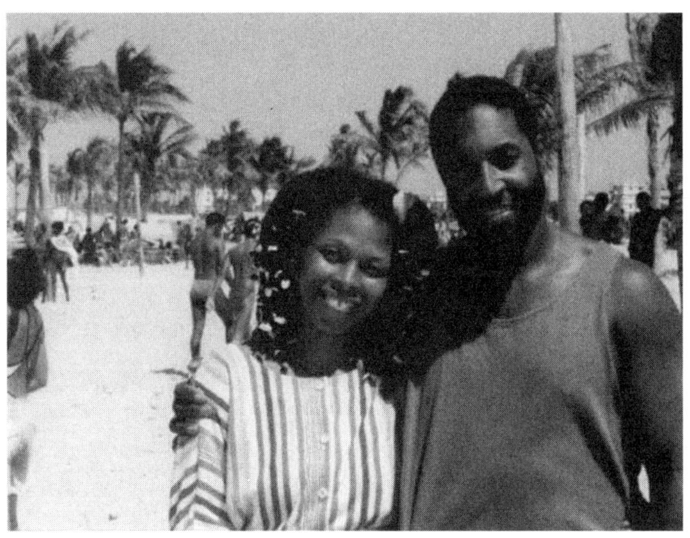

5

YOU CANNOT REFORM THE POLICE IN A POLICE STATE

Antifascist organizing and community control of police

"Black power means the ability to exert a political consequence on the white supremacist construct that is America."

KALONJI: The past decade or so, you've been talking about decentralizing police, community control of public safety, a class action lawsuit against the police and decertifying these unions. I've been in the background cheering you on. It's been rubber to the road all over the country, all over the world. A whole lot of these so-called activists and freedom fighters, they heard the same thing. Why do you feel it hasn't taken hold, for one? What are the main issues right now that folks are dealing with, particularly here in Atlanta with the whole Cop City issue.

As an organizer, as a seasoned vet, what would be your vantage point? What would you have done different, or what would you do to strengthen up this particular movement? There's a whole lot of folks who've been charged with domestic terrorism. There's been a murder of an activist out there, one of the forest defenders. The Atlanta city council basically told over two hundred people to kiss their ass. We're talking about building a Black united front. Is that possible in this era under the current conditions and the particular activists that are out here today?

DHORUBA: Historically, when the Black Panther Party called for a United Front Against Fascism in '69, we used the word fascism in the united front. The reason why we used the word fascism is because we understood, at that particular time in 1969–71, the pushback against the so-called Civil Rights Movement in the South that had achieved voting rights and desegregated schools was at its core white supremacist, imperialist, and genocidal at home and abroad. You had the Vietnam War and Black soldiers coming home who felt that, like Geronimo Pratt, they had to take stand and fight for something other than Uncle Sam.[1]

The right wing, the so-called military-industrial complex, was on its back foot because of the embarrassment of the Vietnam War and the popular resistance to it. The right wing, the so-called political elite, hadn't consolidated their power. They were on their back foot in 1969 and '70 and then throughout the '70s. When the Black Panther Party called for a United Front, it was to consolidate the peace movement, the anti-war movement, and the Rainbow Coalition with other movements in this country. You've got to remember, at that time, the Republican Party didn't have its so-called radical wing that evolved after this period, the so-called Tea Party. All of these were reactions to the gains of working people.

When we called for this United Front, it was at the right time in the right moment to delay this consolidation of white supremacy's new political paradigm of manipulation. Today, though, the right is consolidated. It's been strengthened by post-9/11 laws that permit law enforcement to do things that would have been declared illegal by the Church Committee when it was investigating COINTELPRO and excesses of the US intelligence and police agencies, especially the FBI.

We dropped the ball in that sense, because the United Front, when we organized it, we had in mind a strategic vision that all of those organizations and individuals that came from all over the country will go back to their individual cities and set up local National Committees to Combat Fascism chapters. In these chapters, they would begin to organize and mobilize people to combat police terrorism and the occupation in our community, and put decentralization of police and community control of law enforcement on the ballot.

In New York that's what we did. In other areas, that's what we did. When a movement is encapsulated like it was a few years ago in the wake of George Floyd and the other killings, then the types of

1 Geronimo Pratt, army veteran serving two tours in Vietnam, was Minister of Defense of the Los Angeles chapter of the Black Panther Party.

slogans and ideas that come out of that encapsulation are designed to make sure that we stay where we're at, so that it doesn't work. That's why you had "defund the police," the totally asinine, ridiculous idea and notion. Why would you say that and put it out as the slogan? You've got to understand, if we had a genuine movement that had a strategic vision, every slogan we'd use is a slogan designed to express the will of the people and educate the people. That's why we talked about "Power to the People."

Everybody knows what power to the people means, because they ain't had no power. When we said off the pig, everybody knows who the pig was. It wasn't just the police. It was the avaricious landlord. It was the banker. "Pig" was a euphemism for those who oppressed us. What could the police do? Could the police say power to the police? What are they going to say? Off the people? When you have something like "defund the police" and "Black Lives Matter," anybody could use those slogans. They'll tell you blue lives matter. Dogs' lives matter. A roach's life matters. You did that to yourself. If you notice, the leaders of these organizations were invited to the Congressional Black Caucus at the height of their influence when they had the mic. To say what? To define our resistance to the armed agents of the state and how we should approach them, and nothing ever came out of that but the George Floyd reform act. You cannot reform the police in a police state.

We're not in any of these debates. We're not in any of these dialogues about police conduct, and police behavior, and what they are there for and what they do, which brings me back to Cop City. It was the city council that ratified Cop City. It was the city council that was taking this money from corporations that endorsed the police unions. It was the city council that did this to so-called Black elected officials of the community there in Atlanta.

We know, going all the way back to the first mayor of Atlanta, that the Black petty bourgeoisie leadership in Atlanta were always collaborators and conscious agents of the white supremacist state. I'll tell you, I'll say it again, that these Negroes in Atlanta was always full of shit. When Martin died, they all bounced and became elected officials. They all bounced and got into politics. What did they bring? To Atlanta, they brought the Black Mecca. We got the Black Mecca in Atlanta. We got Negroes like Andrew Young. When he was young, he didn't lick boots, too tough. He was more a handkerchief head.

KALONJI: He started licking later?

DHORUBA: Yeah, he was licking later. What I'm trying to say is that these same political elites are the ones who came out of the war on poverty. They came out of the Civil Rights Movement. They punked out of the Civil Rights Movement. Don't get it twisted. When King went down to Memphis to organize for Black sanitation workers and was murdered, all of his crew bounced.

There was no more poor people's campaign. Nobody was riding no mule train. It was Jesse Jackson holding up bloody shirts, talking about the Rainbow Coalition. What was the Rainbow Coalition supposed to do? It was supposed to put Black faces in high places in corporate America.

When Lyndon B. Johnson realized that these cities were burning down every summer, he said, "Well, these niggas ain't got no stake in these places. They don't have nothing near the stairs. We'll do a war on poverty." These were the forerunners of the internet militants. These were the poverty pimps. They were the first ones to identify Black-on-Black crime.

It was the riots and the rebellion that caused the system to have to stop, look, and listen. If people didn't tear up the streets, there would never have been a Congressional Black Caucus. These poverty pimps, segued into politics, that became the Jesse's and all of these individuals that wound up in the Congressional Black Caucus. Their descendants wound up being totally irrelevant to the entire process of Black liberation. When we talk about something like Cop City, we have to understand that if my first proposition was correct—that the police are armed agents of the state—then it means that the idea of Cop City was to train armed agents of the state.

Now, these armed agents of the state work internationally with other armed agents of the state, particularly the Israelis and the European Union. The US trains with Israeli agents and Shin Beth agents. The NYPD has an office in Tel Aviv.

There's this close symbiotic relationship between US law enforcement and other right-wing hunters, whether it's Egypt or whether it's in South America. We know the whole history of the death squads in South America and how they were trained by American law enforcement. The same thing with Haiti. The former police chief in New York went to Haiti, after Aristide was removed, to train the Haitian police.

If that city council was seriously a product of Black empowerment in Atlanta, of grassroots working people's political expression, they would have never voted for Cop City.

KALONJI: You're talking about Cop City and you mentioned Andrew Young. Now, I don't know if you're aware, but GILEE, the Georgia International Law Enforcement Exchange, is on Georgia State campus: it's strategically located in the Andrew Young Law Building at Georgia State University. GILEE, the exchange between Israel and Georgia police, has existed on that campus for thirty years. It is in the Andrew Young building, so if anyone is confused. . . .

DHORUBA: How poetic.

KALONJI: How poetic.

DHORUBA: That's poetic.

[They laugh.]

KALONJI: That's as gangsta as you want to be right there.

DHORUBA: They have institutional memory, and because of that they're able to create the struggles of today. They're able to manipulate and encapsulate the struggles of today. I pointed out all that stuff about the Congressional Black Caucus in the war on poverty, because all of these things led in sequence, the war on drugs, the war on poverty and the war on crime. The war on crime was the pretext of militarization.

The war on drugs was the pretext of mass incarceration. The war on poverty was to create a Black capitalist entrepreneurial class that would advocate the Boyce Watkins crew, the "Keep the dollar in the Black community," and "buy Black" and all that crap. Each one of these so-called wars that the government instituted brought forth the agents that we have today who are running shit.

If we had a city council that had put a referendum in ten years ago for community control of public safety in Georgia, in Atlanta, where we had a Black mayor, where we had a Black city council, where we had a Black population, where we had Black businessmen, where we have Black football teams, we had all this Black shit right there, we couldn't control the po-po?

KALONJI: We talked about this ten years ago. The sad thing about it is, in the immortal words of Gil Scott-Heron, "It ain't no new thing." This is what we were pushing for with all those police terrorism panels we did, the rallies, the protests, the press conferences, and a lot of these folks were there.

DHORUBA: You didn't have the money of the funding agencies and the funding-industrial complex. You didn't have Soros' money; you know what I mean? When you look at the height of the so-called Black Lives Matter movement, everybody was throwing money at them. Millions. They weren't throwing no nickels and dimes. They were throwing ten million here, five million there.

KALONJI: Make it rain, yeah.

DHORUBA: Yeah. Now, you and me out there talking about community control or public safety with an umbrella in the rain, that wasn't happening, bro.

KALONJI: I know.

DHORUBA: People would look at us and say, damn, man. I ain't get involved in the struggle to do bad.

KALONJI: Right.

DHORUBA: Y'all shoes got paper in the bottom.

KALONJI: I know.

DHORUBA: [Laughs] But then again, here comes Slick Willie. Here they come. They clean. They in their slick ride talking about crime don't pay.

KALONJI: Right. [Laughs.]

DHORUBA: Crime don't pay, and nobody is above the law. That's why it's in the Andrew Young Law Center.

KALONJI: Amen.

DHORUBA: I'm just saying if we had followed through, if that movement was a legitimate movement that was legitimately talking about organizing a united front that could segue into a third political party. . . . You ought to understand, the purpose of the United Front wasn't just to decentralize the police. It was to bring together the New Left so that we could form a political party to influence debates and issues.

KALONJI: I'm not even going to go back to the '60s. I'm going to keep it in this decade. If folks would've hopped on board back when we were popping this in 2010, 2009, 2008, do you think that there would even be an argument around a Cop City?

DHORUBA: No.

KALONJI: It wouldn't even exist.

DHORUBA: No.

KALONJI: The community control would be settled already.

DHORUBA: Even if you lost the battle for community control because the police unions had more money than us, even if we lost the battle, they would never open their mouth again about a Cop City. They just barely got by. They would say, phew, we just barely beat that by the skin of that chinny chin-chin. Let's not rile that back up again.

But you don't have that. You have a bunch of individuals on the city council, you understand, who have bought into the notion of the American century, the American dream, the American exceptionality.

The United States is a white supremacy nation state, and this nation state is ruled by the gun, this nation state is a police state. Therefore, anything that smacks of police control of the political system would be anathema to that city council person, so they would've never even thought about voting for Cop City. They'd be trying to say, look, if we need anything, we need a training ground over there, you understand, so that we could train all the young people on how to be better community managers.

They would be talking about how we need to have our own response apparatus so that we could intervene in the domestic sphere, so we could intervene in these gangbanging disputes, so that we could intervene in these things with respect from those who we are intervening with. How are you going to do that when the people have never been educated to the true role of the police?

All they do is figure out that the police got guns and they will kill you. They will shoot you, so you might as well just keep it moving and try not to get involved with these crackers, because they don't mean you no good. That's it. That's how it is.

KALONJI: You talk about community control, and that sounds like a foreign thing. Every day, we talk about Black power. I think even that particular term has been watered down. I don't think that folks really understand what was being said when we talk about Black power. I think Black power is becoming slowly—if we allow it to—another form of sloganeering or fashionable militancy, just pure rhetoric. What is Black power as you know it and what should we be doing?

DHORUBA: The first thing is that the poor people—Black people—don't mourn. They need to get even. That's the first version. Following that is that Black power means that for those who transgress against our community and our people, there will be a political consequence. That consequence will not be something that they would be comfortable with or that they would be willing to have to suffer under. Now, I know in the beginning, crackers are going to be feeling all ill and stuff and feel that they could just beat us down, but you know how we roll. Black don't crack.

We really need to understand that Black power means the ability to exert a political consequence on the white supremacist construct that is America when it infringes on our freedom, on our humanity, and on our right to self-determination. That's what Black power means to me. Black power can be encapsulated, can be used to obscure the class nature of our community. There are Black enemies of Black people. There are brothers and sisters who don't mean us well. They only mean themselves well. They will do anything to maintain that type of influence or position. They'll use this rhetoric of Black power in order to maintain themselves. Real Black power means that we have to have the ability to exert a political consequence on our enemy, a real serious consequence. That was the basis, or that was the auspices of the Black Liberation Army.

I believe it was Amílcar Cabral who said that you can tell the potential for liberation of the people by how much their culture is differentiated from the culture of their oppressors. Those weren't his exact words, but he was saying that people cannot liberate themselves if their culture is so similar to the oppressor's culture that it's almost indistinguishable.

One of the problems that we have in the diaspora, especially in the US, is that we identify almost completely with the concept and the idea of white supremacy European nation states, such as the United States of America. The USA is a racist construct. It was a white supremacist construct from its very inception. Therefore, the racial component that circumscribes and encompasses the class differences in this society are very acute, very pronounced.

I just wanted to say that, without a revolutionary culture, it's impossible to carry forward a revolutionary movement or a revolutionary struggle. The best that we could hope for in the United States at this particular juncture of "American Empire"—the United States is an empire—is that we could bring forth a generation of abolitionists who are dedicated to abolishing structures of white supremacists' power and white supremacists' nature of the national security state, rather than reform those institutions and make them more palpable to Black people and our so-called Black leaders.

KALONJI: I want to touch on the summer of 2020. We heard the rallying cry, everybody yelling, "Defund the police, defund the police, defund the police!" Let's talk about decentralization of the police, man. Can you rap to us about that a little bit and why folks should jump behind the whole decentralization?

DHORUBA: We've already been there and did that with the police. How do you think the Civilian Complaint Review Board became an institutional tool of mismanagement and oppression in Black communities and a useless organ of protest? They were the counter to the decentralization of the police. The Civilian Complaint Review Board was created by the police unions. When people say "defund the police," they don't know what they're talking about. The capitalist state—the white supremacist state—needs the organized armed agents of the state in order to maintain power. That's what they are. They're not workers. The police are not workers, they're armed agents of the state. Therefore, they have no right to even have a union. Yet, they have a union, so they use that in order to poach labor rights and to make it look like they're workers and that they should have workplace safety and all of that. Their workplace is in our community. If they don't live in our community, how are they working? How are they policing it? They're policing it as an occupying force, they're policing it as armed agents of the state and have proven themselves hostile to the interests of African people and Black people, not only in the United States but globally.

We need to really understand that defunding the police is an oxymoron. It's a stupid statement. It's a redundant statement. That's why they're able to talk about a John Lewis anti-police law enforcement bill, or whatever, that puts money into police departments for better training. Now, instead of them beating your ass to death, telling you "don't resist," they'll choke your ass to death, telling you they're not holding your throat.

How many times are we going to have this same fight? How many times are we going to talk about voting rights again? How many times are we going to revisit this shit? Come on, man. When we have young people who don't understand their radical history and don't relate to their radical traditions and don't understand exactly how far we've come, they would popularize slogans like "defund the police." Anybody that studied fascism and studied the police state or authoritarian states will know that the police are not going to be defunded by the elite. If anything, they're going to give them more money. That's exactly why when you elect a senile cracker like Biden to the presidency, raise them up because you say, "Well, he's better than Trump and he makes white folks feel comfortable" because he's a semi-senile old man. He comes out with this real militant rhetoric about he ain't defunding nothing, in fact, he's going to give them more money and they're going to get more military equipment.

So, we need to really understand what this means—that America is run and controlled by white men with guns. You can't make it no simpler than that. You haven't got a Black politician in America that doesn't have to appease the police unions in order to get elected. He has to be tough on law and order. He has to be a supporter of these major reactionary right-wing police associations and unions.

The police have more political clout in Congress and in local affairs than the Black community does with the plethora of Black leaders that we do have in America today. We have more Black leaders, more Black elected officials in office than we've ever had in our history, and we have less power. We have no political control over the armed agents of the state.

When you talk about defunding the police, you are talking about police departments in some cities that are larger than some United States Army battalions. They're armed with military-style weaponry and they've been training with some of the most reactionary and racist police forces in the world. The police departments of the United States have the same domestic function as the US military abroad. They are there to police, are in our communities, and in our cities to "serve and protect," to serve the interests of the rich and the property owners, and protect their property and interest in our community. They're not in our community to serve and protect us.

Fighting crime is only incidental to their major function. Their major function is to protect the system and the power elite that controls this capitalist system. If we understand that, then we understand basically that the armed agents of the state, the police are not workers. They're not ordinary consumers. They are armed agents of the state. They enjoy the privileges and extra privileges of unionization, of collective bargaining. Although they can't go on strike. They're forbidden to go on strike and that tells you right there, that they're not workers. Workers can strike. Workers can demand wage changes and changes in their condition of employment. The police can't do that. They have devised different methodologies to show their displeasure whenever there's political decisions that affect them. They have the Blue flu. They got work stoppages, but they can't go on strike.

They're talking about defunding them? You're talking about a police department that has an annual budget of $40 million That's modest. Out of that $40 million, let's say you take $20 million and you put it into homelessness and into other childcare and all that. Then they've still got $20 million in guns and armored tanks and property rights and are still going to trump your human rights.

You have to change your relationship to the police. Public safety has to come from the communities that they police. We have to have community policing districts that are based on our assessment of what needs to be enforced in the community. We need to have community control of the police, and we need to decentralize their command-and-control leadership. In order to do that, you have to break the back of the police union. You have to break the back of the national police union. You have to show that the police are armed agents of the state, and that the state is a white supremacist construct. Therefore, the police's job is to support and maintain the construct of white supremacy and inequality in the United States, pure and simple.

The reason why I'm bringing this to this point is that when we talk about how we rethink policing in America, it's not just about reforming these institutions. It's about abolishing them.

When we say abolishing them, people say, "Well, you got to have police. You got to have some type of mechanisms of control in society. Otherwise, people go buck wild and kill each other, and there's no accountability."

When we talk about abolishing policing, what we're talking about is abolishing the political control of the armed agents of the state over the social and political development in our community and our safety. We're not talking about abolishing public safety. We're talking about changing the nature of public safety to make it more socialist oriented, making it more amenable to the conditions of the people that they're policing.

They're trying to do this with various programs now. The police know what time it is. They know the writing's on the wall. They're coming out with these innovative so-called reforms now, where they have psychiatrists and social workers being deployed with police units, and all of this stuff. That's not changing the relationship between the police and the state. The police in America are the armed agents of white supremacy. They're the armed agents of the national security state, and so they are not workers.

If we want to begin to change the face of policing in America, we have to understand that that's their role, and we have to go straight ahead and have these police unions decertified. We should build a national movement to decertify these five or six major police unions. It's the police unions, in the final analysis, that exert the political power in our communities that have them killing us and getting away with murder, that have them enjoying so-called qualified immunity, and all of these different extra constitutional privileges that they enjoy. They enjoy these privileges because they have the power of life and death in their hands because they are armed agents of the state.

KALONJI: When you talk about abolition, what are the limitations? You have some folks that are confused into thinking that when you're talking abolition that you are talking about possibly only going as far as Frederick Douglass or asking for permission to be released. When you say, "And go straight ahead," when you're talking about decertification of the police associations and unions, and whatnot, what does that mean in layman's terms?

DHORUBA: Well, what it means is, when we talk about something as simple as community control of police, this is not just having a community activists and community leaders sitting on some community civilian complaint review board, reviewing. That's not what we're talking about. The same way that the right and white supremacist organizations like the Republican Party gerrymandered political districts, so that they could control the votes of Black people, and minorities, so-called national minorities in any given area. They do that so they can stay in power.

When we talk about community control and police, we're talking about districts where the community elects and selects their own public safety officers, the ones that control public safety in their community. This doesn't abolish the police learning how to police professionally, going to police academies, and learning the techniques of policing and maintaining civilian law and civilian order. We're not talking about just no cops on the streets at all, and everybody just running buck wild, that's not what's being said here.

What's being said is that if the police are armed agents of the state, then they don't have our interests at heart. They have the state's interests at heart. We know that corporate money and corporate funding control the politics of America. They control both political parties in America. We don't have an independent political party. Therefore, we don't have grassroots organizations that are independent of the influence of the Democratic and Republican parties. Every Negro that is in the Democratic Party is there to protect themselves, to protect their own interests, to protect their power. They're not in the Democratic Party to actually protect the power of the Black community, because we don't have no political party. We don't have a third political force. We are subjected to the paradigms and the definitions of our oppressors: the Republican and Democratic parties.

So, having said that, when we talk about community control of police and decentralization of police, we know that in most urban areas, the police chief is appointed by the mayor or the head of the city council. So, the mayor picks someone from the ranks of the police department to be his armed goon. He's the one that controls the police in the city. That police chief determines the so-called discipline and organization of policing.

This is what we have in New York, we have a former cop that's the mayor. He's bringing back all of the policies and all of the programs that failed in the past, and he's talking about, "This time, we're going to put a police jacket on the undercover cops, so that when they kill you now, when they pull you over, and they murder you, they got a jacket on, so you was able to identify them," but nothing has changed.

When we talk about community control of policies, we're talking about each district, whether it's congressional, whether it's a local district, has its own public safety board, a public safety officer, who then commands the police in that district. Every neighborhood and every city has different needs for policing. Some neighborhoods may have an uptick in drugs and drug trafficking. They require a certain type of policing. Other neighborhoods might be less, or they might be more residential, and they might suffer from break-ins, and house robberies, and burglaries. That's another type of policing. The community needs to determine the policing policies in their community, be able to fire and hire police, be able to censor police misconduct.

There should be residency clauses for the police, at least for the first few years after they graduate from the academy, they should live in the community that they were assigned to and police, which means that housing has to be set aside for public safety. Public safety personnel, public safety officers, will be able to get affordable housing in the communities that they police.

Whereas such a policy may not be feasible in a commercial area. We have a downtown area, where there's stores and there's shops, and there's actually nobody living there. That's a whole different type of policing.

What I'm getting at, is that when we think of community control of police, we think about the police as being those individuals in the community who live with us, who have to undergo the same types of problems that everybody else does. That's not possible with a union that's run by these rabid racists. Most of these individuals who are running these unions are rabid racists and right-wing zealots who view crime and violence as an excuse to mobilize themselves militarily, to get more guns, more support for murders, for so-called controlling violent felons. When you have a cop come in to New York and say there's an uptick in gun violence in the city, now they're going to deploy cops to search people's backpacks on the subways, to stop people in the streets and question them. All of your civil rights are being curtailed in this effort to curtail crime.

We know that most of the stop-and-frisk, most of the killings of innocent, unarmed Black people, have occurred over minor violations—traffic light violations, tail light out, speeding, jaywalking, selling loosies—all of these things that don't require a cracker with a nine-millimeter who, after he blows your brains out, tells you he was "scared to death."

The person he shot was on unarmed, but he still shot him fifteen times at point-blank range. Or he was running away when he shot him, yet the cop still feared for his life. If he's that much of a bitch-ass punk, you don't need to be a cop.

We really need to understand that recruiting policemen should be part of the community process, the community should be involved in this. We need to understand that policing comes from the community. The Constitution talks about a well-regulated militia that the people should raise. That's what the Second Amendment is supposed to be about, but the only ones to recognize the Second Amendment in those terms is white folks, and they recognize it to protect their white privilege.

This is why in America you see a right-wing that's armed to the teeth, it has political power, and they have infiltrated the police and military. In the Black community, we're talking about gun buybacks, but we also know that for the past twenty years, stop-and-frisk gave hundreds of thousands of young Black men and women criminal records to prevent them from even owning a weapon, because of those little charges on their record.

The Black community is completely vulnerable to the violence of white supremacy, both extrajudicial and judicial, and we have no way to defend ourselves. When we talk about an abolitionist movement, we're talking about a movement that abolishes the ability or the power of the police to murder us, to intimidate us, to control us, and take that control into our hands.

Abolition doesn't mean the abolishment of law enforcement; it means that we take control of our own communities and enforce the law ourselves in a fair and equitable terms. That the courts and everything that follow behind that has to be radically changed.

When we talk about abolition, we're talking about abolishing the white supremacist's construct that created policing in America, that created the judiciary in America. Rather than reforming these institutions, which in my view cannot be reformed, because that's not their purpose, that's not why they were created. They were created to control us. They were created to dominate us, and it was created to suppress working-class interests. You can't reform that because you don't have the type of wealth and control of labor that would be required to bring about fundamental, institutional reforms.

If we want to really talk about deconstructing the police, we have to understand why the police are necessary at this point in history to somebody like Trump or to the corporations of America. Why are they necessary now? Fascism is the context in which the necessity evolves, because fascism cannot exist without a national security state and without an authoritarian form of government that has a national police force at its disposal. From the day we were brought here, the African community in the United States has been living under a version of fascism. We have this Frankenstein version of fascism here in America, because we have the merger of democracy—so-called democratic institutions—with the corporate, militarized state. Fascism has always been the marriage or the unity between finance capital, the rich, corporations and the state. It's the state that has the monopoly on violence. It's the state that can legally kill people literally. It's the state that can control dissent. Without a national police force, fascism is almost impossible.

When we look at the history of fascism, its rise to power in Italy, its rise to power in Germany, there were differences, the Brownshirts that Hitler had, he had to translate them into the police. The way he did that was to weaken the regular gendarmes, the regular police, merge them into the fascist party, and out of that came the national police force that Hitler needed, as well as the Gestapo, the political police—they can roughly be compared to the FBI because they were the ones to kick people's doors in for whispering antifascist statements, and stuff like this.

We have to understand that fascism has always emerged from the right, and it has always emerged as an instrument of the rich and the industrialists to control the economy and the military of state. If we really look at fascism and how it rose to power in the '30s, almost all of the major US corporations during Hitler's rise to power and even after he was in power, supported Hitler. Ford supported Hitler, JP Morgan supported Hitler, and IBM was the one that offered strategic technology services to the Nazi regime.

What I'm trying to say is that fascism controls the national security state through finance capital. That's the essence of it. It cannot operate, it cannot manifest itself without the type of political control of the masses that only an authoritarian figure or a delusional system of democracy can provide. Historically, fascism has always eliminated any type of democratic expression. The fascism of Italy grew out the workers movement, the Fascista Party grew out of the workers movement in Italy, and the rest is history.

The Nazis rose to power, Hitler came to power in '33 with the pretext of staving off a communist and socialist takeover, and the threat of anarchy when the Reichstag burned down. Hindenburg then gave Hitler the right to rule by decree. Fascism has always come out of the right, and has always squashed democratic and socialist movements. Here today, though, because we don't really have a democratic system here, we have an Electoral College system which does not reflect direct democracy. It's not like a parliamentary system. Here, the winner takes all. In the parliamentary system, you have a shadow government or whoever got the most amount of votes in the minority, they can form a shadow government. They can be critical of the individuals in power. Although I have my beefs about the limitations of that being really democratic, nonetheless, it's much more direct. One person, one vote is much more in play in a parliamentary system than it is in the Electoral College system here in America. Having said that, we've had two or three presidents in our lifetimes who won the Electoral College and lost the majority vote. Each one of these presidents has turned out to be real right-wing pieces of shit.

We need to understand that we don't have a truly democratic system, but now when you impose the new religion of corporate finance capital, and that's the new theology of the West: capitalism. We see these huge office buildings that says, "Finch and so-and-so." They're like cathedrals. What we're dealing with here is a little different. Democracy still exists on paper, the electoral system, but fascism is in full effect. What is that? It's democratic fascism.

It is democratic because it has the bogus pretense of being a democracy with the Electoral College system, when in fact, it's a dictatorship of property. The Electoral College system came into existence because the former slaveholders, the landed gentry, those who had property wanted to ensure that after they passed the so-called Declaration of Independence, which stated that all men were created equal, they wouldn't risk losing their properties. They said, "Wait, man, if we're all created equal, they might take our property. They keep these slaves here. What are we going to do about that?" "I tell you what we do, we'll make the vote based on the population in each particular area. We'll count the n*ggers as three-fifths of a human being so every slave master could have a vote. If you put two, three-fifths together, we got six-fifths. We got an extra vote plus a fifth." You see. Don't get it twisted now. That shit worked. It's been working. The census doesn't say you're in prison in Upstate New York. It just says that you live in Upstate New York. The people in Harlem don't claim their brother that's in Attica as being in their household.

KALONJI: How might the BPP have dealt with today's situation?

DHORUBA: If it were around today, I think that given the Black Panther Party's ideology and the way it was going, one of the things that we would do is we would not sit back and throw out meaningless phrases that we have to that give the enemy oxygen to co-op the legitimate movement of people. Like, "Hands up, don't shoot," and "defund the police." The intentions are good. I understand that the young folks want to use these terms because they reflect what they think at the moment. But because they haven't studied the history, they haven't understood that we already won this battle.

That's why you have the Civilian Complaint Review Boards, which was the co-optation of the idea and the notion of decentralization of police. That's what the unions use to get around the more radical proposition of community control of police and decentralization of local law enforcement. That's what they use.

The Civilian Complaint Review Board has been instituted in over fifty cities across the United States, and none of the rates of murder of Black people have diminished. In fact, these Civilian

Complaint Review Boards have done little to stop the police brutality in our community and hold the police accountable.

We need to understand that in 1968 and '69 the Black Panther Party already won the ideological and political struggle to decentralize the police. We already won it, and we had referendums on the ballot. But it was the police union that flipped it to get meaningless reforms.

Just like we hear today now, how Biden says he's not for defunding the police. In fact, he's been giving them more money in order to train them and sensitize them. It's the same playbook. If those radicals today, those kids on the street today, understood that we have already won, they will be trying to organize a national referendum on police unions. They should be talking about filing a class action to recertify policing agencies, because it's the police unions that influence the political climate in the communities that affect law enforcement. They're the ones that the mayor appoints in most cities, the city council appoints the police chief. Therefore, it's a political consideration to the estimate, and he can't upset the unions. The unions have organized themselves and put money into legislation to terrorize the Black community, to militarize the police, and the unions are strong.

The fact of the matter is that the police are not workers. The police are not ordinary working-class citizens, they are armed agents of the state. They've arrested over thirty-five thousand activists since June [2020] who were out in the streets, first behind George Floyd. They have arrested most of the leaders and a lot of these activists. They charged them with serious crimes, some of them felonies like disrupting national commerce, blocking interstate highways, all of these things. They're charging them with these crimes, and most of these kids haven't spent a minute in jail before. The minute they go up into one of these penitentiaries or one of these holding cells, they're terrified. They're intimidated. All of that rah-rah shit that they talked about in the streets, when the guns are drawn and they in the joint and they're stripped down and they in a stripped cell and ain't got no toilet paper and they got this cracker got to come and give them toilet paper to wipe their ass, now they're scared. Now they start to think their politics through. Having been there and done that, that's the time your shit's supposed to get more serious, not less accommodating.

We need to really understand that we have to organize our communities to survive. This is a new era. This is a new time with new technology. We're living in a global village. We're living in a time where instant communications determine a lot of our thinking, where perception is reality. Fake news becomes very, very crucial in mobilizing and organizing people. It was Dr. Huey P. Newton who said, "The power of the people is the ability to define phenomena, and make these phenomena act in a desired manner." If we can't even define what's happening to us, we come up with slogans like "defund the police."

That's not to mean that the brothers and sisters who thought of that weren't sincere. They just didn't think it through in the heat of struggle. They knew that the cops had all this military equipment. It was a military program that was giving surplus military equipment to the police. The police were using this military equipment to do what? Occupy the Black community and intimidate us, just like the Black Panther Party said they would. The way to stop this is what? Defund them? Just take some money from them? That's the way to stop it? I think the LAPD budget is over $3 billion. What, you take $150 million from them, that's going to change how they police us? We take $150 million and we build a daycare center, we build a community center for the kids? We start a baseball team and the police will stop murdering us, that's how it works? No.

You need funds to run a movement. You need resources and we could use Marcus Garvey for an example, where he had the largest organized Black movement in the history of Black America and he didn't get no funding. The Black Panther Party didn't get no real funding, although we weren't opposed to kicking in doors and confronting crackers and taking the money. If you're not opposed to that. The BLA, we know we expropriated money from the financial institutions. We need to understand there's many methods in which the masses of people can finance their movements themselves, but the most important methodology of financing the movement and building resources is the organization of the masses of Black people in their community.

Once we do that, we'll find out there's nothing that we cannot achieve. The breakfast program didn't rely on funding from Soros. He was probably a kid then. It didn't rely on funding from the state. It relied on us. We'll go into the groceries, into the white stores, Black stores in our community who was selling food to our children's families, to say you need to donate some of your surplus food, some of the stuff you're going to throw out at the end of the week because it's spoiled. You need to donate this to the church now. We didn't say give it to us. We said we got this program in Bartholomew Baptist Church and we feed forty kids every day. We need eggs. You got eggs. Of course, if you don't contribute, all your eggs going to get busted.

Who were the robber barons? Where did Carnegie get his money from? Where did Ford get his money from? They were busting unions. They were busting heads. They stole it from the labor of ordinary working people.

When we point to past struggles and analyze the victories achieved by previous generations of Africans in the diaspora, especially the United States, it not absolute victories that we referred to, but significant battles and struggles for recognition of poor and Black and disenfranchised peoples that moved forward the parameters and legal restrictions imposed on oppressed people and their political and social existence.

For example, when African people, colonized for centuries and exploited by European imperialism engaged in anticolonial armed struggle and won "national Independence," they achieved relative victories, but the global system of geopolitical capitalist imperialism remained intact. Indeed, European imperialism assumed a new and more insidious dimension of control and exploitation of former colonized people with capitalist globalization, or what I call "New Age Imperialism." Kwame Nkrumah, the first President of independent Ghana pointed this out in his book, *Neocolonialism: The Last Stage of Imperialism.* Clearly, every contradiction has a limitation, and every limitation creates new contradictions with their own implicitly new limitations. In the case of African nations created in the crucible of nineteenth and twentieth century decolonization, it was the post-WWII international Community of Nations, and the geopolitical power of the United States and its Allies that led Nkrumah to say, on the eve of Ghana's independence in 1957, "The Independence of Ghana was meaningless without out the total independence and unity of Africa." His words ring true today, as Africa still struggles to control the benefits of its own resources and exercise freedom from Western dominance.

Similarly, in the mid-twentieth century, when the so-called Black Civil Rights Movement succeeded, through nonviolent protests to force the white supremacist settler state of America to reform its "voting rights laws" with the Voting Rights Act of 1965, it was victory for a People whose very humanity was enshrined in the Constitution of the United States as "three-fifths" of a human being in order to enhance voting power of Southern slave-holding aristocracy. Despite the seeming "victory" of the voting rights act (as symbolic as it were), Black People in white supremacist America today are still fighting for unimpeded access to the voting polls. Clearly the Voting Rights Act didn't end racist impediments to Black electoral empowerment.

Again, when the American democratic fascism and the burgeoning militarized police state we have today began its consolidation as the push back of Nixon's "Silent Majority" against the Black Power Movement, and to constrain Black political insurgency to superficial reforms during the decade of the seventies, white America's legal and executive branches of government did so by capitalizing on white fears of crime, drugs, immigration, and seething urban unrest in America's domestic, predominantly Black, colonial enclaves we now flippantly call the "hood." The "War on Drugs" and "War on Crime" set the stage for the emergence of an entirely new Black political comprador class comprised primarily of antipoverty pimps and middle-class Black apologists who championed the neoliberal euphemistic "War on Poverty" of President Lyndon Bains Johnson and his successors Nixon and Reagan, and so on. The notion of "Black capitalism" as the key to Black empowerment gained ascendency especially among the Black middle class hungry for a slice of the white corporate America's cherry pie. The results of this right-wing pushback was mass incarceration, a new Jim Crow containment for the impoverished class of Black people historically marginalized by institutional white supremacy. Did white America benefit from this duplicitous underhanded subversion of the Voting Rights Act of 1965, and derailment of Black radicalism? Absolutely! Currently there are more "Black" faces in high places than at any period in American history. The system of right-wing racist power, masquerading as "neoliberalism," employed Black proxies to legitimize institutional white power, sanction the War on Crime, the War on Drugs, and support restrictive immigration policies.

When the Black Panther Party, riding on the upsurge of antiracist Black militancy in 1968 succeeded in putting forward "community control" of the racist armed agents of the state—the police—on a citywide referendum in that year's statewide election, the Police Union spent millions to convince New York's electorate that a "Civilian Complaint Review Board" on which the mayor of New York could place "community" civilians to vet complaints arising from police misconduct was more appropriate than community control over public safety. Was a civilian complaint review board a victory that reigned in police terrorism in the Black community? Absolutely not. Is public control of policing still a struggle? Well, the emergence of "Cop Cities" around the nation tells us that it is.

KALONJI: Definitely, we appreciate you. Dare to struggle, dare to win. Stay ready. You won't have to get ready. Free 'em all.

DHORUBA: Thanks for having me on, peace bro!

MANDELA IS FREE. FREE ALL POLITICAL PRISONERS!
"It's been said that there are no strangers in the struggle for freedom, only comrades that never met. Black political prisoners of the United States share a human experience with you that few who have not undergone long periods of imprisonment, isolation and torture for their political principles can understand. Amandla!"
— from a statement by Dhoruba Bin-Wahad on behalf of U.S. political prisoners. Dhoruba greeted Nelson Mandela at his appearance in Harlem. Dhoruba, a former member of the New York Black Panther Party, spent nearly 19 years in prison fighting frame-up charges of assault on a police officer. He was recently released when the charges were overturned.

6

THE LIMITATIONS OF A HASHTAG MOVEMENT

Leadership by victimhood and organizing for power

"In the white supremacist culture of the United States of America, white folks don't mind and Black folks don't matter."

KALONJI: Here we are, over fifty years after the Panther 21 case, and while we're talking about the Black Panther Party, there's a whole different type of movement on the streets right now. I want to speak to that because we know all the things that the BPP went through. We know the things that the BLA went through and all the things that RNA and SNCC and so many other freedom fighters who were out there putting in the work went through. Of course, nowadays we have an era where you have "leadership by victimhood." Then we also have what we call "grave robbers," who pretty much step on a scene and reap the benefits of those who were assassinated or those whose children were lost in this particular struggle. What do you see now as far as accountability and responsibility is concerned? Is there a big difference, in your opinion, between what went on with you all and what's going on in the "hashtag movement?"

DHORUBA: History never repeats itself. You've heard me say that many times. History never repeats itself, but it does rhyme. The same conditions could arise, but they arrive at a different time with different influences on the masses. The masses of the people basically always simply determine the success or failure of any type of revolutionary change.

That has been skewered a bit by technology. The advent of instant communication has made the world a global village. It has connected all of us and in ways that we haven't anticipated. This is especially true with social media, because perception is reality to many people in this day and age. Not necessarily the truth, not facts, but perception. This leaves the field open to internet gangsters, network militants, charlatans, and these types of folks who have a vast audience, a wide audience. The face-to-face relationship that revolutionaries had to have back in the '60s and '70s when Black power was declared in the South by Willie Ricks and Stokely Carmichael is really absent.

I think you should understand this when a hashtag movement like Black Lives Matter comes along. I know people are going to say, "Well, Black Lives Matter was not really a hashtag movement. It was a movement of young people who were tired of police murder and police brutality in our community. It took to the streets in the wake of the most egregious of crimes that could be imagined." But how did we wind up with that term? How did we wind up with a hashtag becoming the name of a movement? The reason Black Lives Matter came into existence was because of mass media and social media. It wasn't because the brothers in Ferguson and the sisters who were throwing Molotov cocktails back at crackers were holding press conferences. They weren't; they were being characterized as criminals and as thugs.

Black Lives Matter started out as a hashtag after the Trayvon Martin miscarriage of justice. If we look at the players who were involved in that miscarriage, we see the same players that were involved in that miscarriage are also involved on the George Floyd team. The same players that were involved in the Michael Brown affair. It was those Boulé Negroes, those anti-poverty pimps, the ones that were professional grant writers who were running programs—and many of these programs were very progressive programs, don't get it twisted, many of these people were doing sincere work in the community, helping at-risk families, homeless people—these people had an understanding of mass media and they were the ones that flooded into Ferguson and set up press conferences and started defining the issues. They knew how to operate and use social media.

The founders themselves, they came out and voiced their outrage after the murder of Trayvon Martin, but Mike Brown's case in Ferguson was, however, the first time these activists actually hijacked the movement. Just the first time that they actually were the ones doing the press conferences. They were the ones who, while the young folks at Ferguson were out in the streets, demonstrating and throwing tear gas back and forth, burning down the QuikTrip, and protesting in the streets, brought the whole issue to national attention. These individuals had expertise. They're very intelligent. They were outraged. I'm not saying that they didn't go into that as legitimate activists, I'm saying that they went in with a certain expertise, a certain experience, certain connections, and they were able to amplify that with the white media. It was the white media that took the hashtag and began to label it the "Black Lives Matter" movement.

It were the victims who became the icons of the movement and, in fact, laid the basis for the likes of Al Sharpton to come in to create movements based on victimhood, leadership by victimhood. We have hashtag movements and leadership by victimhood.

We are fighting for justice for Breonna Taylor or for George Floyd as if they could benefit from this justice. They're dead. If they would've had some benefit from mass participation, it would have been when that cracker was kneeling on George Floyd's neck if somebody's thrown a brick at that cracker and ran so maybe he would've got off his neck. Maybe he turned away and George Floyd might be alive today.

Now, his family is going to get up there, pushed up there by Sharpton. His family is apolitical, ain't had a political thought all their lives, and now they're thrust into the maelstrom of a movement because their kin was murdered so violently, so brutally, so nakedly on television that everybody in the world said, "Man, that's how they kneel on my neck. Black lives *do* matter, let's get out in the street." They got out in the street. What did the family stand up there and say, "Oh, George wouldn't have wanted violence." If George would have gotten somebody violent when that cracker was kneeling on his neck, he would have loved it. "Get him off my neck somebody, please. Get him off my neck." If somebody would have thrown their camera at him rather than photographing, he might still be alive today.

What we're talking about is that we have been so programmed that we would watch our own brutally murdered on television, on camera, and not do nothing about it. But we're not fighting for victims. We demand treatment for human beings. Not as cattle. Not as chattel slaves. Not as hounds. We're fighting for liberation. When we articulate this revolutionary fashion in terms of a

Black Liberation Movement, as opposed to a Black Lives Matter movement. . . . When in America did Black lives matter? Did you remember that? Can you remember when the last time Black lives mattered in America? Huh?

KALONJI: Not since America began.

DHORUBA: It was always mind over matter. It's really ironic that what passed for a movement—the Black Lives Matter movement—used the term "Black lives matter" when in the white supremacist culture of the United States of America, white folks don't mind and Black folks don't matter. I don't know why would you name a movement "Black Lives Matter" when we know that capitalism and white supremacy does not—and cannot—value people of color, does not value Black lives, does not value Black people, and does not value the poor and working class. Why would we name the movement after a structurally impossible aspiration? The fact that they would say "Black lives matter" and use that as a hashtag to signify a movement limited their analysis and power, and sucked up all the oxygen of a genuine movement, and then after it sucked up all the oxygen, after the enemy was consolidated around this opposition, then the leadership bounced and went on to live their best lives.

The purpose for the naming of a hashtag movement is to encompass or facilitate encapsulation. We must understand the tactic of counterrevolutionary politics and the use of encapsulation of organizations by the state. Encapsulation is a process by which the enemy—those in power—create movements that they can control and direct and siphon off the energy and the power of those who want to really do something in a revolutionary fashion, who really want to contribute to a real abolitionist movement. It's a known strategy to encapsulate a movement by centering organizations and individuals that seem to personify what the movement stands for. We see that many of the so-called activists that were in the streets back in June and July have become the foremost advocates of electoral politics. The hashtag movement has become a means of encapsulating the rage and the righteous struggle for power that Black people should be initiating. It has hijacked an entire generation's understanding of their militant and radical history.

It's because this generation is not in touch with their radical and militant history that we are having this fog cast right now. They have no historical consciousness and no connection to the actual movement, that's why they don't even know there are political prisoners who have spent all their lives in jail for exactly what they're out in the street fighting for. I'm talking about Romaine "Chip" Fitzgerald, who was in jail for fifty-one years before finally dying in captivity in 2021, and about Sundiata Acoli, who is going on eighty-five when he was granted parole in 2022. This generation doesn't even know they exist. There are young Black women running around with T-shirts saying "Assata taught me," and who do not know that Sundiata Acoli has been in prison since Assata was captured. What is it? "Assata taught me" is written on the front, and "Sundiata I forgot" is on the back?

We still have a number of Black political prisoners still in prison, still suffering, like Imam Jamil Al-Amin—H. Rap Brown—who gave the name to a whole genre of music, rap music. Don't act like rap music came out of a political vacuum. They passed an interstate law to incite riots and named it the Rap Brown Law. We need to understand that it's not the same today because of technology. It's not the same today because this generation is not in touch with their radical history and radical legacy. This generation does not understand that the struggles that they're fighting today we've already won.

It's things like this that tell us that the leadership of a movement that doesn't understand the connection to their own history is a bogus leadership. If it does not attach itself to the people's struggle for liberation and for freedom, what is it representing? It's representing reform. It's representing a way to make white supremacy more powerful to us. What are they actually fighting for? If you have a movement that does not declare itself a Black Liberation Movement but instead declares itself a Black Lives Matter movement, then the enemy has all this oxygen to say, "Well white lives matter, police lives matter. Why do Black people have to have more consideration than anybody else?" You left that door open. If you said it was a Black Liberation Movement, half of these niggas with no sorrows in them wouldn't have donated no money, we know that. If you said it was a Black Liberation Movement and you were in solidarity with other peoples' movement in Palestine, in Africa and in Asia, you weren't getting no money from Soros and Amazon. You could forget that part.

If we have hashtag movements, we're going to wind up endorsing a Democratic candidate. We're going to wind up talking about the lesser of two evils. We're going to try and become a social service agency for the government. We're going to wind up taking Ford Foundation grants and thinking that we're liberating our communities. Why are we renaming bills after bootlickers in order to curb police violence in our community? Why don't we have community-controlled local police, a decentralization of police power? Why haven't we taken over the command-and-control structure of law enforcement? Law enforcement's primary function and purpose under capitalism is to carry out the rule and the mandate of the most powerful class in society. That's why property rights are more important than human rights. That's why we can say we can't breathe, and them crackers don't care because they'll suck up all the air and they'll pollute worse than ever. Whatever is left after, that they will sell it back to your Black ass. We need to understand that only if we have an abolitionist movement—a liberation movement—are we talking about being in touch with our heritage and overturning the system of white supremacy.

We need to really seriously understand that this is the age of mass information and what you don't know, will get your Black ass killed. What you do know, you have to act on. If we know that we've already won, why haven't we consolidated our power? Why don't we have a Black political party? Why don't we have a Third World political party that's an insurgency party that's about the abolishment of white supremacy in its totality, not reform, not modification, not administrative change, but abolishment? We're right back where we started with point number seven in the Black Panther Party program: "We want power and we want the ability to define the destiny of the Black community. We want an end to police brutality and the racist occupation of our community."

We're right back where we started. This is the season of the switch and we're right back where we began.

KALONJI: When we're talking about defunding the police, I remember some years ago, we were on a panel with the Civilian Complaint Review Board in Atlanta. They had no answers to anything. They were toothless. In fact, I don't know if you remember, they put up some billboards out here talking about, "Don't run." Then he had, "Oh, hands up, don't shoot," and the dire situation.

Why do you feel that this whole sloganeering thing is thought of as a solution, opposed to what it is?

DHORUBA: Any social movement that's aimed at empowering masses of people or mobilizing masses of people uses slogans to simplify the ideas behind that movement. Everybody on the progressive side could use it. They could say "Power to the People," "Black power to Black people," "Brown power to Brown people," "working-class power," "power to workers." These things could be used. Popularizing slogans is a form of simplifying ideas in a strategic vision of a coherent people's movement.

This generation has not been in touch with their own radical history, so what they do when a Black man is murdered with his hands up, is that they think, "Well, hands up, don't shoot." They fail to realize that hands up is the universal sign of surrender. If you're marching down the street with your hands up and you're saying, "Don't shoot," you've already surrendered.

KALONJI: Right, you lost.

DHORUBA: Yeah. You're basically saying, "I got my hands up, don't shoot," when we know that the police will shoot you with your hands up, so what's the point? It's a generation that doesn't understand the value of slogans in mass movements.

The opposition has to get ahead of the movement. To get ahead of it, it has to define what the goals are to get ahead of it. One of the things that we've learned from revolutionary struggles historically, is that we have to make a distinction between ourselves and what we owe. We have to make a clear line of distinction, so that the people will understand what we advocate and what we stand for, as opposed to what the enemy is advocating and what they stand for. Now, when you blur those lines with superfluous slogans like "Hands up, don't shoot," that's an emotional response to somebody that was murdered with their hands up. I can understand the emotions behind, but you don't make that into a movement slogan, because that's the universal sign of surrender. Hands up, don't shoot, and you get shot anyway. That's what they call a willful crime.

If we really felt that our lives matter, and this is who is trying to convince me, we'd shoot back. We will let them crackers know that my life matters, and if there is going to be funerals, there is going to be funerals on both sides. If we're going to have democracy in America, we are going to have a democratic distribution of this pain.

Without a democratic distribution of pain, there is no possibility for justice in the courts. We're the only ones suffering, we're the only ones getting shot. We're told, "Don't run away." We were told not to run away during the bullwhip and slavery days. The crackers said, "You better not run away." It is going to be worse. It is like, "Feet, don't fail me now." I am out of here. "Knees, move for me."

KALONJI: Chop my foot off, I'm still running.

DHORUBA: Hobbling on one foot. You see what I am saying? We're told not to run. We're told to put our hands up. "Don't make no sudden moves." You see this in the cowboy movies, in *Tombstone*. "OK, partner, don't make no sudden moves now." You understand? You know how the slick kid on the block, the new gunslinger, he would make fake moves to his gun to get the old man to draw so he could shoot him down. This is what these crackers do.

KALONJI: You remind me of my grandfather with that. He told me back in the day, he said, "Look, always carry two knives. What you do, drop one on the ground so when they reach to get it, you go ahead and open them up."

[They laugh.]

DHORUBA: He made sense. What I'm getting at, slogans are very important to any mass movement. Slogans should be really thought out. Not some spontaneous emotional response in the moment. A movement that's led by victims has never been successful. When you look at South Africa, when the students were murdered in Soweto the ANC's ranks swelled. Where did the kids go? They left to get trained by the ANC, and those that remained, they fought back to build up the infrastructure against apartheid. Everybody suffered in Soweto. The families of those children, but you didn't see the mother of the daughter that was killed in Soweto getting up talking about, "Oh, what we need to sit down with the system, and get the pass law lifted." No! They had a movement to fight. That movement was inspired, was galvanized by the treatment of their children, by the murder of their children, and by the ruthless apartheid regime.

That's what George Floyd was. It was an inspiration for a whole generation of people that said, "I'm not going to be the victim no more." We know for fact, the minute that the victim decides that he's not going to be a victim no more, it's a whole different movement. He's no longer a victim. Now, he's active in his own liberation. We need to understand that, yeah, Emmett Till was a victim. I remember Emmett Till's open coffin on *Jet* magazine to this very day. It was 1955, I think I must've been eleven, twelve, something like that. I had no politics like this at all then. But that picture . . . I ain't never forgot that picture. His mama opened that coffin for that precise reason, "Don't forget what they did to my son!" That started a movement. She didn't lead it. She wasn't out there, "Aw, I don't want nobody out to get lynched." She didn't do none of that. But when the movement had a victory, it was "Let me bring out Ms. Till." Everybody give her a round of applause because she was the mother of the movement. She knew her place was to inspire people. "Don't let my boy die for nothing," and that's what the movement did. That's exactly what we did. He wasn't going to die for nothing, but now what do we have? The complete opposite.

We have the Sharptons, we have the opportunists now who know the game. Look at the lawyers that George Floyd's family has. They have the same lawyer that Trayvon Martin had. The same lawyer that Mike Brown had, and he ain't won a case yet. He ain't won one case. Now, nobody keeps getting a lawyer to don't win nothing. So, how did he get there? He got there because it's game. Now it's not that I don't want to say that the lawyer is insincere in what he's doing. He's just not doing it well.

Encapsulation of our movement goes hand in hand with physical repression and intimidation, and that's where the armed agents of the state come in. We don't have too many people's lawyers anymore. We have lawyers that, for the most part, are taking on cases and the most that they get is a settlement for the families of those who were murdered. We have lawyers who are not political enough to understand a strategic vision of how to practice law in a way that empowers our people, in a way that brings out the contradictions of the system so that our people could be organized around those contradictions.

KALONJI: Speaking of lawyers, right now, we are in an era where folks think that because there's a settlement, it means victory. But how is it a victory when the people paying taxes and the state is just redistributing what they already took from you? They're not losing anything. They're taking your tax money to pay someone in the community for murdering their family member.

DHORUBA: That tells us then that the armed agents of the state have certain status and privileges over and above any other working-class job or position in society. Not only do they have the power of life and death in their hands, they have the ability to coerce and intimidate people—ordinary citizens—under the color of law.

If that's the case, then the police are not workers. The police are armed agents of the state and they should not enjoy any type of labor consideration as a union, because the union then becomes the political cudgel that protects them, that forces us to have to deal with these settlements. The union provides legal counsel for police who murder us. The unions provide money to put out propaganda and information, and because they're law enforcement, they could also manipulate how witnesses are dealt with, how the community views the issues, because they have enormous influence with the media.

If we have lawyers that are political, they would have come together like we did in the '60s. We had the law commune. We had lawyers that came together in collectives in order to defend the movement, in order to push the envelope of legal resistance to racism and class exploitation. These law communes defended the Panther 21. They defended Geronimo Ji-Jaga Pratt. They defended the political prisoners. They brought lawsuits against the state. Today, we don't have lawyers like that.

KALONJI: What do you feel the difference is? Why do you feel that is?

DHORUBA: The essential nature of this is that we have to educate our community who are locked in to the laws and the status quo. Our people are trying to survive in this so-called legal environment. We're constantly told that no one is above the law. If no one's above the law, then we need to understand what the police unions are. They're a vehicle and mechanism to make sure that the armed agents of the state are above the law.

What should we do? We should bring a class action against the major police unions in the US and recertify them in a way that comports with their role in society as armed agents. The US military doesn't have a union, they're the Army. Why do the police have a union? We need to understand that we're not just talking about an ordinary small state. We're talking about a nation's state that has military-grade law enforcement apparatus. We're talking about a state that has tens of thousands of police.

All of these people are walking around with guns and the power to kill and murder us under the guise of enforcing the law, and they have no restraint. There's no one who could hold them accountable. The union's going to protect them, the courts are going to defer to them, and we don't have no power to do anything else. We do have some power and that power lies in our ability to hold them accountable. We need to hold them legally accountable and hold them accountable in our community. That's why community control of public safety is so important, because it would include residency in our communities, at least for a period of time of probation.

There's a whole lot that goes into public safety, but the mere fact that we bring a suit against these unions, doesn't mean that we're going to win the suit. The educational factor, the ability to have other people now come on to the suit as amicus curiae, as friends of the court, other organizations to bring their analysis and their strategy, whether it's about focusing on conservative racists, or systemic racism in law enforcement.

We could look and understand that this systemic racism in law enforcement is not unique to the US. It's the same in the UK, it's the same in France, it's the same in Belgium. Wherever African people are located as a national minority, where poor people are located as a national minority, where Africans and Arabs who live in Europe are concentrated or have any type of a significant population, the police are straight-up racist dogs, always been that way, whether they speak French, Flemish, or with a British accent.

We have a senile, old man that's a president that'll probably drop dead before the next election. You got somebody like Kamala Harris, who has a lower rating and acceptance rate than Joe Biden.

When we look at the history of Joe, he was down with all of the draconian laws that went into creating the prison industrial complex. He was behind all of the lock-them-up-and-throw-away-the-key laws.

When we look at the last elections, we had a sheepdog named Bernie Sanders, who said all the right things, who was on the right side. I disagree with certain things with him, just like he disagrees with us. He ain't down for reparations, just like the Communist Party USA wasn't down with Black folks the way we needed them to be down. They were down with Black folks the way Moscow had outlined and Marx had delineated. That was the basis of their analysis. When the Communist Party went belly up in Moscow, it went belly up in the US. Now we can go back to DuBois, and Garvey, and see the history of the Communist Party.

What I'm trying to say is that it wasn't the CP or the orthodox left that came up with the idea that we had to have a national United Front Against Fascism. It was the Black Panther Party. It wasn't none of these so-called left organizations, whether they were radical or not, that understood that we had to have community control of public safety and put bills and legislation in, referendums on the ballot, to achieve that end. The enemy understood what that meant, and they countered with civilian complaint review boards.

There's a lot to fascism, and it's not just a simple term, as I've tried to point out. It has evolved with the idea and the notion of the corporate state, and the idea that the corporation has the same rights as any individual. The freedom and style of capitalism that places individuality without responsibility on corporations. If we had a checklist of psychosis and neurotic behavior, and we checked off the individual who behaved like a corporation and the corporations themselves, the corporation would be declared antisocial, sociopaths, and everything.

Having said that, the Black Lives Matter movement and fascism—we're in a historical moment here. Again, history doesn't repeat itself, but it does rhyme. That means that conditions may never evolve the same way, especially after industrialization. We have to understand that human society, and especially Western society, went through a radical change with industrialization that affected every facet of working-class people's lives and of native, Indigenous peoples who had their land stolen. The whole struggle of chattel slavery versus wage slavery versus child slavery was an essential, economic part of the locus for the Civil War. Of course, wage slavery won.

To connect this to the current struggles and the Black Lives Matter movement, the reason why I'm saying "Black liberation matters and not Black lives" is because without power, Black lives, of course, don't matter. It's all relative. With power, however, Black lives have to matter. They have to be considered, because power has to be considered. Right now, Black folks have been, as Amílcar Cabral aptly put it—and I'm paraphrasing—that Black liberation is a return of Black people to the old historical continuum that was interrupted by the European historical continuum. When we go to European history, when we were growing up in school, we always saw that Black people, the African experience was always a footnote. When we look at the US, the current US competition with China, if we go back in history to the turn of the century, we could remember when China was occupied by imperialist powers, and they were pumping opium into the people, and out into the world. Now, we look at this as a completely different thing. The Chinese decided about fifteen to twenty years ago that they were going to lead the tech revolution. They were going to transform Chinese society, and they did. Now they're head-to-head with the US in terms of technology, in terms of geopolitical clout. China is unrecognizable today compared to what it was at the end of 1947.

The reason why I say that, is to say that the Black Lives Matter movement is trying to act as if it is occurring in a vacuum. As if it just went up because someone kneeled on George Floyd's neck. The symbolism of George Floyd, the murder of George Floyd, who was a clear victim of white supremacy and of police racism—institutional racism—has galvanized the whole world. It's because of the crisis of capitalism. It has put other peoples of color and other oppressed people in opposition to their governments, in opposition to the national security state apparatus, which is the model that came out of the industrialization of the West.

KALONJI: Since I've known you, you've been pushing the National Coalition to Combat Fascism. There's been a number of different components that you and the Black Panther Party and the BLA have literally been pushing for a half century. Right now, a whole lot of encapsulations and a whole lot of individuals talk about and pretend to be building on the United Front Against Fascism. It's self-serving.

DHORUBA: Kalonji, you know I feel a lot like you do. We need to understand what fascism really is, that it is essentially the marriage between corporate finance capital and the state. It's a marriage made in hell. This liaison, this relationship, this corporate state structure, this absolute security state structure requires a monopoly on legal violence. It must have armed agents of the state, it has to have a national police force in order to carry through its policies against the working class and against the working people. The problem is that there is no national police force in the US, which means that the only way the government can try and do this is with misinformation and to co-opt genuine leadership.

One of the things that I tried to convey to younger people is that many of the battles that we are fighting today, we've already won. Many of the struggles that we are fighting today, we've already won. The enemy knows we've won those struggles and they have moved the goalposts. They have camouflaged the issues of our victories. They have appropriated our language, our slogans, and everything.

The problem is that the new generation, the younger folks who are coming up and who want to make some types of changes in our community, who want to empower our people, who want to bring about some type of future for themselves, they're not in touch with that radical history. They are not in touch with that. The enemy is. And because they are, they know exactly what they have to do to encapsulate movements today that would revisit the radicalism of yesterday. They know how to do that. Encapsulation is the tactic and strategy of war and of domestic repression.

That takes the energy and the oxygen out of the room, or out of the struggle, out of our militancy, out of our revolutionary fervor. We had political education (PE) classes on a regular basis in the Black Panther Party, not just for those who were cadre and members, but for the community too. We had the PE classes in the middle of the week, which were always open to the community. We've always invited students to come, mothers to come, everybody to come and sit in the political education classes, because raising the consciousness of our people is very, very key and important. Unless we can address that, we don't stand a chance.

Right now, we have the mass media, the weaponization of data, the use of AI, and these various social medias outlets where everybody could individually be a star or get noticed by tens of thousands of people with the click of a mouse. That's very appealing to oppressed people who are marginalized and not noticed by anyone.

The hashtag movement is an emotional response of a generation that sees these blatant acts of racism, white supremacy, and murder, and they try to stand against it. But they don't stand against it based on their history and movement of radical tradition. They're standing in order to get along. They don't have no comprehension that the Black Liberation Movement in the '60s had concrete relationships with the people in Palestine, the people in the Congo, with Kwame Nkrumah in Ghana. Kwame Nkrumah put a black star in the middle of the Ghanaian flag because Kwame Nkrumah slept in Harlem. He went to school in a historically Black university. He was schooled by Black nationalists and Garveyites.

We don't have movements that operate from a principled point of view. You could have a small organization, but if they're principled in their politics, if they're principled in their relationship to the people, then they don't have a problem with coalitions and alliances with other organizations who are similarly principled. We may not agree on everything, but we're not talking about uniformity here. We're talking about unity.

We have a myriad of examples of united fronts and revolutionary struggles to draw from, to get lessons from, whether it was the struggles in Africa, whether it was the earlier struggles of working people in America, whether it was the resistance movements in Asia and the Middle East. All of these organizations, all of these movements, whether they were religious, semi-religious, or whatever, they all realized the necessity to broaden their base of support and to appeal to the masses of people in a way that the people could understand what they were trying to do and where they wanted to go.

Back in the day, we were part of a movement. Look at it, too, when we called the first National United Front in 1969, we had Youth Against War and Fascism, which was a white organization. We had Students for a Democratic Society, they were white. We also had so-called hippies, the political hippies, they were white. We also had the Peace and Freedom Party, they were white. We also had the Rainbow Coalition, The Patriots, the Puerto Ricans, the

Chicanos and Indigenous people. All of these people, representing all of these histories.

They all came together in Oakland. Over 2,500 registered and came to formulate a united front against the forces that were pressing against them, after the gains of the civil rights movement in 1969, when the so-called civil rights movement was waning. The war on poverty that LBJ had instituted had created a whole class of poverty pimps. Many of them sitting in the Congressional Black Caucus today. They raised up the whole slogan of "Black on Black crime," in order to deflect from the occupying army of police in the Black community. There was a whole sea change of white liberalism in attempt to deflect and blunt the struggle for Black power at that time.

You remember what happened to King when he first came up to the North and started preaching? People throwing rocks at him, because they had this misconception—I had that misconception, too, at the time, and I ain't going to lie—that when you let somebody beat you up, you was a punk. I realized, of course, much later, that Martin Luther King was far from being a coward. That his strategy, although noble, although humanitarian, his approach to power, he actually renounced it in the end, and said that it was capitalism that was at the core.

This is how King wound up in Memphis, representing garbage workers, Black garbage workers—we're not talking about white garbage workers—we're talking about Black garbage men, you can't get lower than Black garbage men.

How is it that a movement comes along now and doesn't draw on that history? So, these kids that are fighting in the streets, they ain't fighting the right fight. They're motivated by the right thing, but they're not in touch with their own history. We've got Black folks, we've got young Black people all over struggling for homeless mothers, taking over our houses. We've got whole movements in California, in the South, that are vibrant movements, just like Jesse Gray's movement for decent housing in New York led to rent control. We've got young people in the streets who've been fighting against police brutality and police murders in Chicago for the past twenty-five years. We have people that are doing good work in the streets. But they are mobilized and not organized, and without a united front we don't have effect. You're going to reinvent failure When somebody like Al Sharpton talks about another march on

Washington at the end of August, he's talking about building a movement of victimhood, he's talking about a movement that's led by his victims. We're going to have another Million Man March, a Million Woman's March, a Million Grandfather's March, we're going to keep marching and keep marching, and the media who is attached to the establishment, who is attached to the state, is going to keep defining our marches and defining our goals for us. OK? So, they're able to isolate these little struggles, they're able to pick out the individuals in those struggles, go after them and raise up another leadership, just like they did with the gangs. The gangs that came in the wake of the Black Panther Party. Most of those gang leaders had politics, but they are the ones that they threw in jail so that the drug dealers and the straight up, so-called, gangster crew could take power and re-divert any or all of that energy into what we have today.

We have brothers and sisters out there in the middle of a historical movement. They out there shooting each other, and then when we look at this, we understand too, just like we did back in the '60s, that there's a history to this. What did the police do in the '60s? They tried to co-opt and encapsulate the Black Panther Party. They infiltrated it, they had individuals go out and do criminal acts, so they could see what the party was doing.

I just want to end by saying, if you can, folks should just get and read Gwendolyn Brooks, "The Second Sermon on the Warpland." She tells you that it's in the struggle that we are really citizens. It's in this struggle that we are really human beings. Not by declaring ourselves human beings, but by making other people recognize our humanity with our own empowerment.

The things that white folks fear the most are Black people who recognize their humanity and are willing to defend it at all costs, with guns, with or without. That scares white folks because we were never supposed to realize that we were human beings. That's what all this slavery was about. We were three-fifths of a human being. We were not really supposed to read. We were not really supposed to write. We ain't supposed to think for ourselves. We were supposed to do none of that. When we realized our humanity and we say, "We are not going to let you oppress me. That if you shoot at me, I will shoot back. That if you are wearing a blue costume and you think you going to inflict the justice on me, I'm going to inflict revolutionary justice on you. There's going to be funerals on both sides, not just on my side."

We try to devise all of these mechanisms and all of these strategies to make white folks feel good about themselves, and therefore grant us a contract with humanity. We make movies about how we got to make white people feel comfortable. We don't understand how that works geopolitically. How that's a detriment to us exercising our right to political power, our sovereignty. We don't think as a sovereign people. We think as a minority, as a national minority who's been wronged by society, by white society. Therefore, if we're given a chance, we could be just good as everybody else at doing what white folks do. Instead. we celebrate the first Negro this and the first Negro this. We're still celebrating firsts.

KALONJI: We celebrate the ass whoopings, too.

DHORUBA: Absolutely, and because of that, we have become incapable of thinking independently in our own interest. We feel that if we think in our own interest, we've got to consider everybody else's attitude and their interests. I grew up on a mantra that when people mess over you, you don't get mad, you get even.

When's the last time we got even? When's the last time we held these people to account and said, "If you do this to our community, this is what is going to happen to you, and you don't want that." If we look at the Europeans, the colonizers and the Americans, they have never gone anywhere to take over anything that you didn't have to kick their ass before they left to make them leave.

KALONJI: Then meanwhile back at the ranch, folks are gunned down regularly and we still blame the victim. . . .

DHORUBA: Why didn't he follow instructions?

KALONJI: Right. Why did he throw his hands up? Who told him to go to sleep in that car?

DHORUBA: The people that say that is the same ones that would have been snitching on the plantation that we were going to run away. We let him know. Yeah, they would say, "Jabo over there. He's going to run away tomorrow night. Can I get a little more of them pig feet? He out of here tomorrow." This is the same thing today. "Why don't you cooperate? Why did you do this? Why didn't you do that?"

KALONJI: "He told you not to run."

DHORUBA: "Yeah, he told you not to run. What you running for if you didn't do nothing?"

KALONJI: "Why did you pull your pants up?"

DHORUBA: Well, you know you can't run if your pants is down, which has some practicality or you wear flip flops. You see what I'm saying? The point is that we have accepted our role as victims. We've accepted our role as eternal victims. We have movements led by victimhood. That's what makes it so pathetic, because the enemy knows that. America knows that. They know that. This is why they make jokes out. "Is it because I'm Black?" That's a joke now. You see what I'm saying?

They have reduced our oppression to self-flagellation. We don't need white supremacy to tell us that we have no power. We do it to ourselves, because the minute that one of us gets into a beef, the gun is drawn. Then right when the crackers come along, everybody throw their gun under the car.

KALONJI: We've seen some of these characters literally. When they see pigs coming, put their guns on the hood or put their guns on top of the damn roof of the car, the top of the car and back away. "I got a legal gun." You know what I'm saying? I mean it is crazy.

DHORUBA: Yeah, because the terror that has been inculcated in white society since its inception was Black men with guns. That has been a terror. Every plantation owner had that terror, that their slaves were going to rise up, slide in, cut their throat, and chop their head off. If you look at the Civil War, Black Union soldiers were never captured. They were killed when they were captured. They were mutilated and murdered.

When a Black man fought for what he thought was his freedom against the Confederates, he knew that he might not get out of that alive. If he got captured, he might as well save that last bullet for himself, because they were going to torture him, they were going to kill him.

We don't understand that the idea and the notion of Black self-defense is translated by white society into terrorism, into adherence to Black terrorism and Black racism, or hatred of white people. It has nothing to do with hating white people. It has to do with loving yourself and despising white supremacy and the privileges that ensue, that come from white supremacy.

That's why we've got to have a democratic distribution of the pain, and that's real democracy in a white supremacist society. A democratic distribution of the pain. That's what we need right now. Crackers need to feel the pain that we feel, and that's what's going to bring them to the negotiating table. That's what brought them to the negotiating table in Vietnam. That's why Kissinger and Le Duc Tho both got a Nobel Peace Prize. That's why de Klerk and Mandela both got a Peace Prize because there was equal distribution of the pain.

We ain't the only ones that are supposed to feel this. We ain't only ones supposed to be calling for our mama with a cracker kneeling on our neck. They need to go to funerals, too. They need to mourn for their loved ones, too, and understand that we have this humanity together on this planet and at this point and at this time. You're not going to take my humanity from me under no circumstances. That's why I tell these kids in the streets, "You are right. You all stay in the streets. If you don't stay in the streets, they won't change nothing."

But you have to understand that your presence in the street is not going to change things in and of itself. You have to make sure that there's a consequence for everything that they do to us.

There should be a consequence for George Floyd. That's how the BLA came into existence. It exerted the political consequence. You kill one of us, we will whack you. We will hunt you down, and we will whack your ass. Now, we might go to jail. You might kill us. Hey, ain't nobody getting out of this life alive. I didn't expect to live this long. I never expected to see any of this. Now that I see it, I'm happy. I'm glad, but I realized that these kids are about to reinvent failure because they don't have no connection to their history and the enemy does. The enemy knows what it's doing, and they don't. That doesn't mean that the answer isn't there. They just have to organize.

We shouldn't mourn George Floyd; we need to organize. We need to organize for power. If we're not organizing for power, and we're just talking about how, "Oh, I'm oppressed because I'm a Black woman, and the Black man is more oppressive to me than the white man," come on, man. If white supremacy isn't personal, then misogyny isn't personal neither. Misogyny's part of a system. Nobody was born misogynist, hating on women. We were made that way. We were socialized into that behavior. If we were socialized into that behavior, we could be socialized out of it. The only way that we can be socialized out of it quickly is to overthrow the system that supports it, that maintains it. It grows fat off of that misogyny. That's capitalism. That's the system right now that we are representing. It's not something that's separate and apart from this. It's all part of the same thing.

7

SOLDIERS' STORIES

A conversation with BLA veterans Sekou Odinga, Thomas "Blood" McCreary, and Dhoruba Bin Wahad[1]

DR. JARED BALL: What's up, everybody? Welcome to this very special edition of Black Power Media's look at "A Soldier's Story" in the Black Liberation Army history. I'm Jared Ball here with my crew—Kalonji Jama Changa and Kamau Franklin.

Welcome to the everybody. Especially, welcome to our very special guests, Sekou Odinga, Thomas Blood McCreary, and Dhoruba Bin Wahad.

DHORUBA: First of all, I want to thank you, Jared, and the Black Power Media, Kalonji, and Kamau, for keeping it real, and getting our story out to real radical tradition.

I want to talk about the Black Liberation Army, but I want Sekou to talk about some of the things, especially the international section of the Black Panther Party and the BLA, how we have the solidarity with the armed struggles of others in Africa, like in Guinea Bissau and the Congo, as well as the Palestinians. This is the history that belongs to our people. Also, I want to mention how the BLA was part and parcel of the BPP's Ten Point program, especially when it came to military service. In the BPP program and platform it says that, "Citizens or members of the Black Panther Party will not be members of any other military army except the Black Liberation Army."

In 1971, COINTELPRO, the counterintelligence program that was aimed at the BPP came to culmination. By this time, the

1 This interview was conducted by Dr. Jared Ball, Kalonji Changa, and Kamau Franklin on May 23, 2021. Thomas "Blood" McCreary became an Ancestor on May 25, 2022. Sekou Odinga made his transition January 12, 2024.

counterintelligence program had devoted over 70 percent of its activities towards the New Left, and over half of that was aimed at the BPP in particular. The idea behind the counterintelligence program was not only to destroy the party, but also to discredit its leadership among the left both in the US and globally in terms of our solidarity movement and our solidarity activities.

By 1971, Huey P. Newton and others believed that they were in danger, that their lives were threatened. This came about as a result of a document that was released by the counterintelligence program, claiming that the Panther 21 rejected the leadership of Huey P. Newton. That, in fact, he was no longer the leader of the revolutionary movements in the US. Huey P. Newton reacted to that. He purged the Panther 21. Much of it is in the documents, but members of the New York 21, myself included, Cetewayo Tabor, Sekou Odinga was already in Africa. He managed to elude the dragnet that was put out to kill or capture him on April 1. He continued his work in North Africa with the BPP's international section.

To the public, the split in the BPP came to light when Huey P. Newton and Eldridge Cleaver did a joint interview on a major television station, and the dispute spilled over to name-calling. The section that Sekou was in was purged from the BPP by Huey P. Newton and his cohorts in the Central Committee. Of course, those of us in the 21 who were out, were in danger of being setup and murdered, so we went underground.

It was the underground, the BLA, that came into notoriety on Malcolm X's birthday in 1971, May 19, when two armed agents of the state were shot. The New York City Police Department launched a campaign to go after the original members of the BPP and the Panther 21 who had been acquitted. This is all in the counterintelligence documents.

Later, I want to talk about the politics of the BLA and why we thought of ourselves as necessary as the underground railroad was to the anti-slavery movement and runaway Africans. We were at war. We felt that our community was occupied by foreign entities, by the armed agents of the state who had no regard for our life and limb—which we still see regularly today. We felt that only with a political consequence we could convey to them understanding that for us, for Black people in the US, democracy was not just an empty word. That true democracy relied on a common sense of humanity. That until white supremacy and the white supremacist organizations that oppressed us understood that, and until there was an equal distribution of the pain, there will be no democratic possibilities or dispensation in America.

Above ground, we talked about the Rainbow Coalition. We talked about bringing all working-class people and poor people and people of color together to form a third political party, to form a force that could be empowered. At the same time, we understood that violence is as American as apple pie as H. Rap Brown, Jamil Al-Amin, said. Therefore, we understood that unless we were able to exact the consequence on the armed agents of the state and those who gave them their commands and orders, they will never consider us a human, they will never deal with us with justice and equality.

That was the basic thrust of the BLA. I really want to turn this over to Sekou, so he could talk about many of the things that the party did and delegations that we sent to the different parts of the world, different parts of Africa. Many people don't even know that we had a delegation that went to North Korea when it was considered a hermit kingdom. I don't know. I believe Sekou went with the delegation, but Sekou could speak better about what was happening with the Black Panther Party internationally.

We were saving Sekou for the last, because that's the best of it, but he could get in here now. Turn this over to Sekou Odinga, my comrade, my brother, and someone I adore and respect immensely. Sekou, you got it, bro.

SEKOU: Power to the people. Free the land.

KALONJI: Power to the people. Free the land.

SEKOU: I think Dhoruba laid it out pretty clearly. The things that I would have to add is what I was involved in particularly. In terms of what we were dealing with, the reasons for the existence of the BLA if you will, was a need for some kind of self-defense. Some sort of consequences to be applied to our enemies, because that occupying force that Dhoruba was talking about came in the uniform of local police departments all over the country. They were, as they continue to do today, attacking us at will. Their doors were always open for white races to join them and to get their particular type of violence out against the Black community as today we see in

Minneapolis with George Floyd and other places, we see these white folks in the police uniforms murdering our people.

We felt that there was a need for a consequence. But to follow Dhoruba's format, let me first say a little bit about the international section of the BPP. It really came about because the then-Minister of Information, Eldridge Cleaver, had gone underground. He went to Cuba and that's where he first tried to start an international section of the BPP, but the Cubans had a different idea of what we should be doing. Their idea was that we should become part of the people and cut sugarcane. That didn't leave us much time to do the work that we wanted to do. We left Cuba and went to Algeria where we were welcomed with open arms.

The Algerian government was a revolutionary government at that time. When they heard what we wanted to do, they not only agreed to allow us to do it, they also agreed to help us do it by giving us a building. They gave us an embassy to work out of and a small stipend every month to help pay the bills, the electric bills, the gas bills, etc. They were very, very helpful and very instrumental in helping us build an international section.

At the time, they did this not only for the BPP, but they did it for all anticolonial, anti-imperialist groups around the world. All the different African liberation struggles from South Africa, from West Africa, from Southeast Africa, all of them were there. You had MPLA there, you had ANC, you had FRELIMO, you had them all, including the PLO. We were all in Algeria, and we were all able to meet with each other openly whenever we wanted to.

We saw our mission over there as gathering information about the struggles going on around the world and getting information about our struggles in the US out to the world. We also sought to build relationships that would help us in our different struggles around the world. In this regard, many of the progressive governments offered help, like the Chinese, Cuban, and obviously the Algerian governments. A number of other governments made it clear that they would help us on the down low, but they didn't want to have no open clash with the US.

Most of our help came from anticolonial organizations. For me, I think I would say that the PLO at that time were our closest comrades. I did a lot of traveling with them myself. I went to the second Palestinian Students' symposium with Field Marshall DC where we delivered a major address of solidarity with the Palestinian people. I believe this was in 1971.

From there, the PLO offered us any aid that they could give us. As you know, they were a struggling anticolonial organization themselves. They didn't have that much. Whatever they had, they opened their doors for any kind of training that they could give us, whether it be with arms, explosives, or whatever. They said, "We're here for you. Come, and we'll give you whatever we can." Some of us took them up on some of that. Basically, that's what we were doing in the international section. We were making contact with other anti-imperialists, anticolonialists, and people who were struggling against the imperialists, the NATO gang led by the US.

Most of the folks out there in those struggles could see the US as leading those who were oppressing them, or aiding those who were oppressing them. They would always tell us, "Whenever you all get it straight over there, it'll be very easy for us to get it straight over here. We need y'all to do whatever y'all can to get them up off your backs because if you get them up off your back, we'll be able to push them off our back real easy."

Without the US support, most of the brothers that were struggling around the world felt that they would be able to easily deal with the local yokels. We were able to make a lot of good contacts and a lot of good coalitions with brothers out there. I traveled with the PLO a lot. I did some traveling through Lebanon, to Palestine, to a few other places. I went into Africa, East Africa, especially.

DHORUBA: Could I just interject something here, Sekou, for the audience. It's very important for people to understand what Sekou was saying about the enormous amount of respect the other liberation movements had for the Black Panther Party, and the Black radical movement in the United States. A lot of folks don't know that in this age of hashtag movements, this is not understood. International solidarity with the Palestinians, with the people in the Congo, with the people around the world was concrete. The NLF (North Vietnamese) offered us concrete assistance, the North Koreans, the revolutionary movements in Africa. It is very important for people to understand that in this day and age with globalization and the US as a new-age empire, the solidarity amongst oppressed people is of paramount importance.

Especially now, as empire begins to transition from fossil fuel to green energy, and the elite and the corporate states are now going to suffer or have to change the deal. Also because of the technological revolution that we're living through right now, with these communications and the weaponization of data. I think people really need to understand what Sekou was saying here, when he talked about all these liberation movements in Algeria at that time, and these liberation movements respected the BPP, and saw us and our people's struggle as one with theirs.

KALONJI: Quick question, Sekou. The time period you're talking about for clarity would be after the Panther 21 case?

SEKOU: Even before the 21 case was over. We started in 1970. We opened the international section of the BPP in 1970 around the summer.

DHORUBA: In New York, right after we tried, remember when we tried the decentralization and community control stuff, Sekou and Blood back in '69. We started a solidarity committee in New York. The BPP chapter had a coordinating committee with other organizations and student groups in New York with the Palestinians students here in America. It was all connected and it was all part of the type of internationalism and anti-imperialism that the BPP exhibited at that time.

This was advanced for Black people. The only other organizations that saw our struggle in these terms was Malcolm X's at first and then actually the BPP, and then Martin Luther King, as we all know, came around to understanding imperialism and capitalism and war in the same manner that we had. Of course, he was assassinated. Yes, international solidarity is crucial to any movement for liberation today.

KAMAU FRANKLIN: We should bring Blood into the conversation. I think for folks who study the history of the Panthers and the BLA, folks get to know Dhoruba and Sekou because you guys have had cases that went public. I don't know a lot of people know Blood's history as much as they should. I was thinking about that the split in the party wasn't necessarily an East Coast-West Coast thing as was popularly portrayed. Can you touch on that a little bit too?

THOMAS "BLOOD" MCCREARY: Yeah. When the split went down, a lot of chapters were expelled around the country. It wasn't East and West Coast because San Francisco went with New York, LA went with New York, and you had other chapters throughout the country that went with New York, so it really wasn't a split. Even today, we still have strong solidarity, especially with the LA chapter.

I think that the COINTELPRO once again portrayed it as a split between the East and West Coast, but that was not the case. We were always welcomed in LA. The LA chapter always welcomed us and many other chapters.

You've got to keep in mind when that so-called split happened, Huey and the rest of the Central Committee moved a lot of people from their locations and closed those chapters and moved them to Oakland. They were getting into politics, running for mayor, running for city councilmen, and that's where they were moving the party to.

Many of us were captured at that time. The BLA went into full swing to say really from '70 to '75. We got captured in '73. That's why I was telling Jared earlier, it's important that we understand that history because it's still portrayed as the East Coast-West Coast thing. As I said, that was not the case.

KAMAU: Would you say it's more of an ideological split?

BLOOD: It was ideological split. Also, it became a bloody confrontation. We lost a lot of people.

DHORUBA: Blood is absolutely right. It wasn't just the East-West dichotomy because a lot of people that came up in the rap game and tried to equivocate Tupac and Biggie, this East Coast-West Coast rivalry of some type of cultural tribalism that exists in the Black community. It's not the case.

Many of the Black people at that time in the BPP, when it first came into existence in 1966 on the West Coast with Huey Newton and Bobby Seale, many of the people who lived there, many of the families that lived there were newly migrated from Texas, from Louisiana, they came there during the war to work and to support the war effort at the piers and the docks.

The Black community in Los Angeles and San Francisco was not as Afrocentric, you might say, much as and tied into the African experience, the African American cultural experience in the North as New York and Chicago and Boston and Philly.

If you notice, Fred Hampton came from Chicago. It's very important to understand that one of the reasons why the New York chapter was portrayed that way, was because the New York chapter was one of the money cows of the BPP, especially after the 21 were arrested.

This was the basis for Lumumba and the brothers in prison believing that the West Coast Central Committee had abandoned them and therefore that discontent was recognized by the counterintelligence program and used to ultimately split the party along the lines of, more of ideology and region than East Coast-West Coast, as Blood was pointing out.

SEKOU: Exactly. Ideologically, the Central Committee was clearly moving to the right and we were holding strong on the left. Blood just mentioned that now, they wanted to run for mayor, they wanted to run for city council. We were a revolutionary organization in our minds, and we continued from that mindset.

It was definitely ideological. We should make no mistake about that, this was not an East Coast-West Coast struggle. As Blood pointed out, a whole lot of those who were expelled by the West Coast Central Committee, were on the West Coast.

People like Geronimo Pratt, Donald Cox—Field Marshall DC—that whole crew, there was a whole lot of them over there that rode with the East Coast if you will, because of the ideological differences and they didn't believe that we needed to go into that type of politics.

DHORUBA: I think that it's very important for the audience to understand just what Sekou said. I haven't really put it in those terms before, but Sekou hit the nail on the head. Huey Newton and the Central Committee were moving to the right.

At that time, people didn't know that the assassination of Fred Hampton in Chicago and the arrest of the 21 and the purging of the 21 were designed to deal with the internal reconstruction of the Black Panther Party Central Committee that we had basically struggled with. Some of us had struggled when Huey got out of prison with the idea that the West Coast was the sole seat of all the leadership of the party, which was now national. They agreed, and we talked about how we would choose the new Central Committee.

One of the things that we understood was, like in the different chapters, like in LA with G, in Chicago with Fred, in Boston with the folks up there, the sister up there in Baltimore, in New York, there were certain brothers and sisters like Lumumba and Sekou himself, who were active in the Pan-African and Black Liberation Movement before they joined the party. They were activists in their respective cities before the party. When the party came to their location, they joined it because of its revolutionary and left nationalist politics, as Sekou was pointing out. From the perspective of the counterintelligence program, this meant that if they let that type of leadership coalesce in the BPP, it would be terrible.

What they did, is that they made sure that Fred got killed. If you notice how Fred got killed, he got killed by an agent who worked for the FBI, the Black desk. If you notice how the Black Panther Party was, the 21 were arrested, and then later Bobby Seale was arrested because of a supposed kidnapping and murder that originated in New York as a consequence of the Panther 21 when they killed Alex Rackley in New Haven. We need to understand that COINTELPRO just didn't kill Fred because he could talk good, because he was charismatic. They went after us because we adhered to the revolutionary line, and those of us who were in New York were in those cadres that pursued that revolutionary agenda.

BLOOD: There's one point that I want to make. When people study the history of the Panthers, you need to keep in mind which era of the BPP you're talking about. The BPP came into being in 1966, and from '66 to '71, I would consider it a revolutionary organization. After the killings started, we didn't touch on that. With the West Coast coming to New York and murdering people out there, we decided that we were going to take the fight to them, but dealing with each other.

That's when the BLA really went into full gear. The propaganda states that we were not known by the community. The community did not support us. That's bullshit. All you had to do after the action happened the night before, is go into any local bar, barber shop, hair salon, and the Black people in those places would be ranting and raving about those brothers and sisters the night before, how they took the fight to the enemy.

They say we were not a part of the Black community. We are a Black community. Where do you think we came from? You understand. We had no problems taking that fight to them, because under the conditions that we were living, especially in New York with them killing kids, throwing motherfuckers off the rooftop, we said, "We cannot go on any longer like that." People stepped up to the plate and started dealing with them. Then I want somebody to change. It's not egotistical.

DHORUBA: Oh, man, distinction to that.

BLOOD: When you took to fight to them, you found out they actually were cowards. They were actually cowards. When the gun battles went down, they weren't performing like they said they were performing, but that's another story. I think that the history of a party has to be understood. It was people in the BPP who came in certain periods in time. If you talk to a lot of people, they don't even know what we're talking about. They don't know that period from '66 up to '70, '71. They talk about 1981. It depends on who you're talking to.

To get the true history of the BPP, it must be told in sections. When the party was active; when it was functioning; and when it became inactive, because I've spoken to Panthers, and it seems like we were coming from two different organizations. It is imperative that you understand the history when people tell you they were in Party, what period are you talking about?

We don't know anything. We had liberation schools in New York, in Harlem and elsewhere, but that was our main focus. We had sickle cell anemia clinics. We had doctors coming in from NYU Medical School and Columbia, who were training people on Wednesday nights. They would turn the office into a clinic, put sheets up. They did their work.

What bothers me is that there's different parts of the party and different periods in time. Because for us in New York, the party only lasted for about three years. From '68 to '70, and in '71 the BLA took over. There was no Black Panther Party, or chapter, really functioning in New York City after '71.

The BLA was out there in the streets. Contrary to what people may think, police brutality decreased once they knew that there was going to be a consequence. That if you go and murder some kids out there, we're going to deal with your ass. If there's going to be wailing in the Black community, we're going to have some wailing in the police officer community. Let them know what pain is really all about.

I consider myself blessed because I've served with some people, man, some of the baddest motherfuckers that ever stepped out of history. I was honored to have been there. I'm going to give you one example, then I'm going to be quiet: Twymon Myers, you need to study his history. He was the same age as Fred Hampton when Fred Hampton died. That brother, when they murdered him, EMS had to pry that nine-millimeter out of his hands. You know what I'm saying? That's how much commitment he had.

DHORUBA: Twymon Myers was a BLA soldier. He was also a community worker in the Black Panther Party before he went underground. He was from the Washington Heights branch of the Committee to Combat Fascism. In 1971, when we were forced underground after the Panther 21 conviction, Twymon Meyers was one of the cadres in the BLA out of New York.

In many ways, Twymon was a very talented young brother in that he was a master at the craft of urban guerrilla warfare. He took to it like a duck to water, and he became legendary. He became someone who the NYPD feared and despised and wanted to kill. He escaped a number of ambushes where he was allegedly surrounded. This is stuff out of a Denzel Washington movie. Man, this young brother. He was not at all physically imposing. If you put glasses on him and a suit, you would think he was a nerd.

Twymon was from the South Bronx. He was from the city. He understood the streets. He understood how to move in the streets. He incorporated that because the BLA was quite territorial in the sense that we were from the hood. It was that we were familiar with our terrain better than the enemy was, better than they were.

Still, they managed to track Twymon. I think it was on 165th Street and Union Avenue in the Bronx. They trapped him one day and surrounded him. They found his safe house, they surrounded him, and they killed him. They gunned him down in the streets.

Twymon was one of many. There was Howard Russell, who was also killed in a confrontation with the police right around the corner from the Black Panther Party office, in fact.

The brother Victor Cumberbatch, who was with him, another comrade in the BLA managed to escape. They were treated by us in our underground hospital.

By the way, just to mention, for the sisters that always talk about Assata Shakur, she came from the same branch and the same chapter as Twymon Meyers. Assata Shakur, though, she wasn't so much a soldier in the sense that Twymon was. She was running our medical facilities underground.

She was a soldier, everybody in the BLA had to have some skills in that respect, but she was a medical cadre. Of course, repression in the system brought us to the point where each one of us had to do a lot of different things. We had a saying that each revolutionary and each BLA member had to be a match for one hundred of the enemy.

We always study, we always try to perfect our techniques, and we always try to develop our political consciousness and understood that what we were doing was not something that everybody was cut out to do, that everybody in the movement couldn't do what we were doing.

Without this component to the movement, the enemy would never take our people seriously, they will continue to brutalize us, they will continue to murder us with impunity, they would never be brought to justice.

Therefore, we had to institute what we would call a revolutionary justice. We felt it was necessary, that when enemies or the people murdered our people, murdered our children, that this had to have a political consequence, there had to be a consequence for this. We felt that this was necessary. That was my generation. That was how I felt, I grew up that way. It was nothing extraordinary about this, as you can tell about the Black Panther Party, it was obviously quite common. I wasn't like an exception to some rule or something here. This is one of the reasons why we fail to realize that without our ability to control the armed agents of the state in our community, we are at the mercy of the state's law enforcement agencies. We have to control them; we have to control them by any means necessary. We have to understand the weaknesses of the enemy, that all politics is local.

JARED: Blood, I'd like to hear a little bit more to the extent you all find possible in this very public setting to talk about the transition from the Panthers to the BLA. How did that happen? What was that like? What of those stories, Blood, that you're talking about that we don't hear, can you share a little bit more of that you feel comfortable and appropriate in this space to share?

KAMAU: Can I add one question, too?

JARED: Sure.

KAMAU: One of the things that people who try to study the BLA talk about, is the structure. A lot of folks hear that the structure was not a "top-down structure" but a cell structure, where folks were given general descriptions of what was supposed to happen. Then, they carried out actions as they thought that they were supposed to do as related to those descriptions. As y'all talk about the development, could you also talk about, as you can, how did structure work for the union?

BLOOD: Let me say this. From my involvement, there was a brother out of Jamaica, Queens, named John Thomas. He took about seventeen kids to Atlanta, Georgia. They rented a farmhouse. In that farmhouse, they trained for months. People became better shooters. Their shit became structured and scientific. Like any young people, once you teach them how to shoot, and they're good on them targets, they get anxious, they want to make moves now. Some people made some moves in Atlanta, it caused a big disruption. People had to scatter across the country.

The structure that I functioned under, we functioned as cells. We made decisions in those cells. We tried to contain it. We wanted it structured, but we didn't want it tight like that. As it turned out, a bank was being expropriated and two cells show up at the same motherfucking bank. We had to have it hooked up where we would have some type of information, what the fuck is going on, because we could get out of the shootout ourselves there.

It was things like that with loose structure, you needed some type of structure. In the beginning it was cool, but then it got outrageous, man. As I said, once you teach young people how to shoot them guns, they want to put it into action, and it wasn't time.

JT was trying to keep a tight rein on them, him being an older brother and have had some experience, and I think he did a good job out of all of his other flaws and shortcomings. That brother did a hell of a job man, because remember, Sekou and Larry Mack, they were gone. They were in Algeria or Cuba or wherever they were at. He was trying to maintain shit, to keep it right.

DHORUBA: When Blood says that, I don't want people to think that the BPP and the BLA went through different phases over the years. Initially because we did have an underground to the party when it was above ground, we always had brothers that functioned more or less in the background. G used to do that before he was brought up to deal with the LA chapter, but we did function as independent cells.

These independent cells, of course, had the same orientation as the BPP in terms of its politics and in terms of its the enemy. They did have tactical initiative and tactical abilities to do what they had to do.

It's very important for people to understand that, our radical tradition was how we organized a legal struggle above ground struggle with an extralegal struggle underground. The same way the US government has its Black Ops, and the CIA has to carry out those things so that the government can plausibly deny that they had anything to do with. It's the same way with a people's movement. And you have to remember that the Black Panther Party had called the year before for a united front against fascism.

One of the things that Sekou and Blood, especially Blood had pointed out, is that there was the Black Panther Party a different phase from 1966 to 1970, whatever. Sekou was talking about how it moved to the right and how they were moving to the right.

It's very important to understand the meaning of the Panther's move to the right after '71. What that really means is that, the Elaine Browns, the David Hilliards were more than just moving to the right in terms of his politics. David Hilliard was probably in all likelihood a source of information for the FBI. The documents seem to indicate that, at least the documents I have in my possession, but that's another show.

JARED: Can I ask you all real quick, because the rightward trajectory that you all suggest of folks out west, at least in part, and you mentioned engaging the electoral/political process, do you three not see any value in that? Is there no radical engagement in electoral politics?

DHORUBA: Yeah, absolutely. Blood and Sekou, we were all there. When the party first started in New York, one of our first projects was decentralization and community control of police. We organized and worked on it, coalesced with other organizations in New York, and got it on the ballot. We got community control on the ballot.

It was the police union who flipped the script and confused the masses of people in New York to vote no if they meant community control, and vote yes if they meant Community Review Board. That's what the politicians in New York, Black and white and the mayor in New York, at the behest of the police union . . . that's how they flipped the referendum.

SEKOU: We were also very involved in the educational struggle here in New York, and in the independent school struggle here in New York, where the people were saying, "No, we want a say in how our children are educated." Then we started moving towards taking that power to educate our own children. It was a real struggle here in New York. That was the real history that needs to be understood.

We always understood that we needed to work within and without the system. We never had known that we would get no work with nobody that's involved with electoral politics. We were not an electoral/political organization. We were not elected. We didn't run for office. I didn't run to be the section leader of the Bronx. I wasn't voted that, they made me that. The committee here, the Central Committee of New York, the leadership in New York did that. We weren't running for office here in New York as the BPP, although we did work with some of the office holders in New York.

KALONJI: I want to say, as the generation under y'all, man! Salute! We are always honored. First of all, it's an honor to even know y'all. Secondly, I fall between comrade and fan, I'm going to just keep it gangsta. Because of folks like el-Hajj Malik el-Shabazz and you all, you know what I mean, you helped us to stay grounded.

One of the things you all have been talking about has been the whole counterinsurgency part of it. We know that it were folks like Gene Roberts, who was involved in Malcolm's situation, and also, I've been told that he was one of the founding members of the New York chapter. Can you all speak to that?

BLOOD: I don't know about Gene being a founder of the New York chapter.

SEKOU: He was not a founding member.

DHORUBA: He wasn't a founding member.

SEKOU: I have to take some responsibility for bringing them knuckleheads like him and Yedwah. What was Yedwah's name?

BLOOD: Ralph White.

DHORUBA: Wait, I don't think you should do that to yourself, Sekou, because I had the security section. Gene Roberts got involved in the security section because Kinshasa brought him there and said he grew up with him, that he knew him, and that he was his homeboy. That's how he wound up being where he was at, at least as far as I met him.

SEKOU: Ralph White walked up to me in the streets in the Bronx and I invited him in myself.

DHORUBA: You could take that responsibility, but Gene Roberts is Kinshasa's.

[They laugh.]

BLOOD: What I have a problem understanding about that history with Gene Roberts, as learned and well-read as most Panthers were, when the Panthers came in New York, why didn't we know that he was Malcolm's bodyguard? Where was he before '68, why didn't we know that history about him? Why didn't he make that known to us?

DHORUBA: Because the radical tradition in New York has always been distorted. The Black radical history and Black radical tradition has always been distorted either by revisionism over time, like you're seeing now with "Judas and the Black Messiah" and with the movies that's coming out on the LA shootout with the Black Panther Party, when the first SWAT team in the US was used against the Los Angeles chapter. We need to understand how they rewrote history. That's why we didn't know up until that point.

SEKOU: No, I disagree with that. He used that as a calling card. That was part of his calling card, that he had been a part of Malcolm's organization. People knew he had been a part. What we didn't know that he was the police in there. That's what we didn't know. We knew he had been in there before.

DHORUBA: Nobody knew that at the time.

SEKOU: Nobody knew that, though. It wasn't that nobody knew that he had been a part of the Organization of African American Unity. That was known, Blood.

BLOOD: I don't want to change the course of this discussion, but when we were talking about politics earlier, Malcolm's widow at Ocean Hill-Brownsville, she was out there protesting for the decentralization of those schools. That was one of the big fights that went on in New York, if you remember that, Ocean Hill-Brownsville.

SEKOU: I remember it very well. I remember you and I were going to go to it together.

DHORUBA: I know you do, Sekou. [Laughs] Your boy Netanyahu and the Jewish Defense League, and that piece of shit Meir Kahane. They were all posted up in New York at that time. They had their own defense committee and their own relationship with the police.

KAMAU: You talked about how there were different phases of both the Panthers and BLA.

There was the second phase with the BLA forming an alliance with members of the Republic of New Afrika and members of the Weather Underground. This became known as "the Family" or whatever.

Can you talk a little bit about this, Sekou? I know you've got to go, but it sounds like this is something you need to hit on a little bit about how that formation came to be. It seemed that before that, there was either a slowdown or there wasn't as much action happening from a BLA point of view. Then came this second series of expropriations and some jailbreaks that happened during that time.

SEKOU: I think you're talking about the development of the BLA. People in the family from present, myself, Lumumba Shakur, and a couple of the other brothers, we were all citizens of the Republic of

New Afrika. I became a conscious citizen of the Republic of New Afrika in 1968.

Going along with what our party demanded was that we couldn't be part of their army. We couldn't be part of their military structure as a citizen. We had that argument with Eldridge and a few other of them when they came to New York when they were saying that we couldn't even be a part of that organization.

Anyhow, there were those in the party who related to land and independence from the start. Those of us who came out of the Organization of Afro-American Unity, those of us who related to that, we heard Malcolm when he said revolution was about land, about bloodshed, and we took that to heart.

When the folks from the RNA organized it, Queen Mother Moore, the Gaidi Brothers from out of Detroit, Imari, and Herman Ferguson. Different people like that. We had our own connection with these people already, people like Dr. Mutulu Shakur. That was a kid that came up under me. I met Dr. Shakur when he was thirteen years old, running behind me, wanting to get involved in stuff.

It wasn't like we reinvented that in the '80s, we just came to light in the '80s. That's when we started to fall. A lot of us got captured in the early '80s. We had been struggling right on through from the '60s. That wasn't stuff that all of sudden happened in the '80s, but we had developed to a higher level of struggle. We had organized some support groups that weren't all New Afrikans. Some of them were European, some of them were Puerto Rican. Specifically, those two, white radicals and Puerto Ricans.

We were able to organize some support committee, some support group out of those communities, that we were able to do some good work with. When you see that in 1981, what they called "the Family," that was something that the media developed. They gave us that name, because we called ourselves a family. We did call ourselves the family, but that wasn't an organizational name. It's just like a group, like a family. We're family.

DHORUBA: Absolutely. People don't understand that New York especially was a hotbed of Black nationalism and radical Black politics. It's always been that way. As Sekou pointed out, he, Lumumba, and Blood, they were all activists before they joined the party. If you notice, most of the activists from New York and from the East Coast had African names, and to those on the West Coast—because they were besieged by likes of that piece of shit, Karenga and the cultural nationalists on the West Coast—they thought everybody with an African name must have been a pork-chop nationalist like Karenga.

Of course, that was a mistake. Having said that, Sekou is absolutely right. We have always had a nationalist tradition, a solidarity tradition. Some of the brothers were even like a Bob Collier, he was in the Statue of Liberty case. He was with the Revolutionary Action Movement.

We need to understand that at that point in '71, before when Kwame Ture left, we met at David Brother's house with Lumumba, I believe Sekou was there. He had just come back from talking to Lumumba's Baba, who was a renowned nationalist in Philadelphia. Zade and Lumumba's father. Sekou know him well.

KALONJI: Was that Sallahudin Shakur?

DHORUBA: Yes. He was a renowned nationalist and he was of a previous generation of Sekou and them. I didn't know him.

BLOOD: One thing Sekou pointed out to me, and I was kind shocked because I didn't know. The brother that was murdered that comes from the RNA.

SEKOU: Who are you talking about?

BLOOD: The brother that was killed with you when he got captured.

SEKOU: Oh, yeah, Utari.

DHORUBA: Utari.

BLOOD: A lot of people did not know that.

SEKOU: He came out of their military. He was with Alajo Adegbalola, who was the first Minister of Defense of the RNA.

KALONJI: Iya Fulani Sunni Ali's father? Is that correct?

SEKOU: Yes, he was.

DHORUBA: I think the lesson to be learned from this is that the struggle that required revolutionary politics and required the type of armed response or the type of extralegal response, was imbued and endowed with revolutionary fervor because of the parent organization they belong to, whether it was the RNA or the BPP.

If we know this, I know people are going to besiege you, Jared, but if you notice, you could judge the Nation of Islam by its fruit. You've never seen the fruit of the Nation of Islam on any frontline struggle. In fact, you've never seen the Nation on any frontline struggle in the civil rights or in the radical movement, they were always self-contained.

They never got involved in that type of politics. They were on that. We need to understand that Sekou was a citizen before he was in the party, we need to understand that this was not an exception. Fred Hampton was in the NAACP in Chicago. You see what I'm saying?

SEKOU: Let me just say this though, because I'm getting ready to leave. I want people to understand that not everyone who was part of BLA was part of the Black Panther Party. It should be made clear, that the BLA came out as a response to the violence of the pigs in our community. The people saw that and wanted to be a part of a response to that. I worked with brothers from Louisiana that knew nothing about the BPP. Had never been even around the BPP, the crew I worked with out of New Orleans.

JARED: Baba Sekou, could you add to your final comments here, anything that you would want to tell people about the resurgence of any attention to Assata Shakur? The "Assata taught me" phenomenon. Sir, could you say a word or two about that too, please?

SEKOU: People always are holding her up and using her quote. I like to tell people that she was part of a movement. She wasn't somebody just out by herself. She was part of a movement. People need to remember that. There are people in prison because of her. Mutulu Shakur, one of his cases is for helping to liberate her. Sundiata Acoli was with her on that highway. No one ever calls his name. No one ever hollers, "Free Sundiata Acoli," an eighty-four-year-old revolutionary who's still standing strong. I talked to him two days ago, he called me. People need to understand that she was part of a movement. If they're going to support her, then they need to support everybody that was part of that movement.

We have political prisoners today that were a part of the same movement that she was a part of. The brother that Blood is talking about, who we're going out to memorialize in a couple of weeks, he was part of that movement. Assata comes out of the BPP movement, out of the Black Liberation Movement. Other brothers and sisters who came out of that movement need the same respect, the same honor that she gets. People ought to give them that, because these brothers and sisters gave their own sacrifice. They lived a life that allows us to live this comfortably as we live today. They pulled some of these pigs up off our asses just like she did.

We have to remember that she's part of a movement. We need to relate to that movement, not just to relate to her as an individual.

JARED: Thank you, Baba Sekou. I just wanted to say, for me, personally, I just want to salute you very much.

SEKOU: Dhoruba, we've got to do this together again, because I would love to sit down with my brothers and just talk some of this history. We've been talking about doing this for a while and haven't done it yet.

BLOOD: You jogged a lot of memory in me, brought things back that were almost gone. I want to say this about the BLA, and people in the BLA not being Panthers. In the cells I worked in, we had individuals, prisoners, who went to jail prior to us, they were training people and sending them to us.

My codefendant was never in the BPP. Woody Green, he was never a Black Panther Party member. They were sent to us from the penitentiary. We need to honor those people.

DHORUBA: A lot of people don't know that the Black Panther Party stopped membership right before the Panther 21 were arrested. Everybody that came into the party was a community worker after that. Assata Shakur, Assata became a member when . . . I actually took her down to the office and had her fill out her membership. Her whole NCCF up on Washington Heights were NCCF community workers, and they were BLA cadre.

SEKOU: Peace. BLA.

DHORUBA: All right, Salamu alaykum, Baba.

SEKOU: Wa'alaykumu salam.

KAMAU: A lot of folks always have questions about some individual Panthers. One of the folks, obviously he died years earlier, but Kuwasi Balagoon often comes up. Can you guys talk a little bit about Balagoon and his work?

BLOOD: He was a soldier's soldier. That motherfucker had respect in the street, believe that.

DHORUBA: He started out in the Yoruba community in Harlem, of all places. He was a cultural activist in Harlem with the Yoruba community there, that would later relocate in South Carolina.

He was a soldier. The first time I met Kuwasi when we opened up the Harlem office. He was living in a squat. He had taken over an apartment building, him and his wife, Ife. They were living in a tenement building that they had taken over with the tenants. They weren't paying rent and they were living in there. It was occupied tenancy.

That was at the height of the tenant strike with Jesse Gray and Mae Mallory in New York.[2] One of the reasons why Kuwasi seems to resonate is the same reason that this generation knows about Assata and doesn't know about Sundiata. They know about an Elaine Brown, but they don't know about Kathleen Cleaver, or they do recognize Kathleen Cleaver, but they assume that Angela Davis was in the Black Panther Party, which she was never a member.

They make all these assumptions because these are Black women. You have a generation of Black women who are being raised that needs she-roes, that needs heroines, that needs a connection to struggle that's not male-oriented. In this age of intersectionality, that's crucial.

---

2 A massive rent strike in New York City erupted in 1964 over the City Council's hearings on rent control and stabilization, spreading across three hundred tenements in Harlem to sixty in the Lower East Side, to forty-five in Bedford-Stuyvesant, and forty-five in the Bronx. The strike, organized by the grassroots Community Council on Housing, had the support of militant unions such as SEIU 1199 of the Hospital Workers of New York.

BLOOD: I wanted to say this about Mae Mallory, she was a revolutionary to her soul. That woman, didn't pick up no gun that I know of, but she taught them sisters in the party how to destroy them big chain grocery stores, by taking a razor blade and just cutting fruit up in there. Mae Mallory was a soldier. Never carried a gun, that I know of, but she taught Afeni and all those people that you can do damage other than picking a firearm.

KALONJI: I'm glad you mentioned Mae Mallory because I was just talking about her a few days ago. When you talk about folks like Mae Mallory and Fulani Sunni Ali, Queen Mother Moore, these are revolutionaries that happen to be women. They're often forgotten about, so I'm glad that you're bigging her up because her work with Robert Williams and so many other people was tantamount.

BLOOD: Oh, yeah. That's just out of Cambridge, Maryland. Malcolm talked of Richardson, Gloria. . . .

KALONJI: Yeah, Gloria Richardson.

DHORUBA: Gloria and Flo Kennedy in New York.

BLOOD: There you go.

DHORUBA: Flo Kennedy in New York, girlfriend was bad. She was the one that mentored Shirley Chisholm on a lot of stuff.

BLOOD: Let me say this shit about the Black community and the BLA: they supported us fully. Most of the people we stayed with weren't in the BLA or other movements, yet they housed us.

DHORUBA: People don't know them to this day, that's right.

BLOOD: When we lost guns out there in them gun battles, they furnished guns to us. The Black community, oh, my God, man! I've been in Florida—no support—they opened their houses up, gave us weapons. The contribution of the Black community to the BLA is unbelievable. They may not have wanted to be identified because of jobs and because of whatever, but they supported us, they definitely did.

KAMAU: How do you respond, then, to the critique that it was too soon for the BLA? The community wasn't ready for it. It was easy for the enemies of Black radicalism or the Black movement to make folks look like they're the boogeyman, all that kind of stuff. How do you respond to the critique that it may not be too soon?

BLOOD: One of those things to keep in mind is that the BLA was supported immensely by the Black community. They gave us housing; they gave us weapons. When we got injured, they kept us moving, man.

DHORUBA: Urban guerrillas depend on the people. That's right. Urban guerrillas and any guerrillas are supposed to be fishing the sea of the people. Isn't that Mao's axiom? You could believe what Blood is saying is true.

We got that way, especially in places like Brooklyn and Manhattan, because when we were selling papers in the community, when we were out in the community, Abdul, Blood, we'd be sitting up there playing checkers and stuff in the community with the pastors, drinking wine. We were in the pool halls and all of that stuff.

When we went underground, we still had that rapport in the community. The people knew that we were for real. The people knew that. I'm going to end with this. To this day, there are people who helped the BLA that nobody knows about. I want to give a shout out to all of these old-school people who are out there listening.

BLOOD: The unsung heroes. Have you ever seen that movie, "21 Bridges" about New York? Any rate. We were locked down in New York and couldn't get out for two weeks. The women that put us in the trunk of a car and drove us to Cleveland, they were bank tellers. They didn't know a damn thing about the BLA. It's an eight-hour drive. They went out there, Sunday night, we arrived, came by the trunk. They had some food and got back on the road, went to New York. We couldn't have done that because all the activists were monitored, them that was not out there, so we had to depend upon those people.

There are people in the BPP who had those connections, who never went underground. They kept us moving. We couldn't have survived without them, but people getting shot, man. We had a doctor, he's dead now. They had a saying about him. If you can get to him, you got 90 percent chance of surviving your wound.

DHORUBA: When Victor and some other folks got shot, we had people in Harlem Hospital that would lend us the instruments and the tools and even the facility on the DL if we needed it. That's important because we know the gunshots wounds got to be reported to the police. How do we survive? It was the masses of people, power to the people.

BLOOD: There are people who've been wounded, seriously wounded. Doctors working in these hospitals, "Get him to a motel, and we'll keep him alive." They did that and went back to work and did their business. They are unsung heroes. He's dead now. What's his name? Burke, Alan Burke, out of Brooklyn, white doctor. If that doctor, if it hadn't been for him and people like Prime who had four or five gunshot wounds, when they did the autopsy, old wounds. The support that so many people offered. It makes me think about Harriet Tubman. All the people on the Underground Railroad who lent their help and whatnot. We don't know about them people.

KALONJI: This reminds me of Che Guevara when he was talking about being in Bolivia. People, when you talk about guerrilla warfare and whatnot, guerrilla warfare is not you walking around with a whole bunch of equipment. You need the help of the people.

Che talked about how folks would leave food out in pots hanging outside of their homes, so when they passed by, they'll have something to eat, you know what I mean? Definitely a shout-out to those folks.

Sekou served, what, thirty-three or thirty-four years in prison, Dhoruba another nineteen. To have these brothers on BPM right now is an honor. That's one of the reasons we need to support political prisoners, because of the fact that they're coming out, they can come out.

JARED: I've got to say, man, forgive the interruption, but seeing Blood smoking cigarettes on the porch reminds me of the story I've always read of John Horse, one of the few revolutionaries to make it and live out his old age on his porch. I feel like I'm getting to talk to John Horse. [Laughs] I love seeing it. I love it.

BLOOD: You know what Assata Shakur used to say about Sundiata before they got busted? She'd say, "Sundiata looks like somebody's grandfather." We were sitting on a porch somewhere, Sundiata with a pipe in his mouth. Looks are deceiving.

We survived that way. There are certain individuals who couldn't drive cars on highways because of their demeanor. There were a lot of motherfuckers with frowns on their face, they wouldn't let them go through the toll booth, driving through the toll booth.

[They laugh.]

KALONJI: That would be Dhoruba.

[They laugh.]

KALONJI: I've got Dhoruba's stories, too, we'll come back to at another date, in different states, I'm trying to tell y'all.
DHORUBA: I've got juju working for me. If I drive a vehicle, I'm driving. . . .

KALONJI: 120 miles an hour.

DHORUBA: If I'm doing 120 miles an hour in a red Mustang. . . .

KALONJI: Going through Mississippi.

DHORUBA: In a red Mustang, going through Mississippi, with dreadlocks, them cracker police will look at me and they see a rabbi driving a limousine.

KALONJI: I ain't feel like no rabbi in the backseat, I'm going to tell you that right now. [Laughs.]

DHORUBA: That's that camo. You know that cloak defense that they got in *Star Wars*, where they cloak the ship. I got that.

KAMAU: The idea about the expropriations, particularly of banks, that just takes a lot of bravery and forethought. Obviously, the reason to do is that's where the money is. The fact that you all developed the ideas around, "Look, we need to fund revolutionary activity in different ways." Go into what you can, of course, doing that work.

DHORUBA: Let me say this, Blood and I never robbed a bank in our life. We never expropriated anything from anybody. We always believed in the BPP's legacy and program to take not one single needle from the masses of people.

Now, having said that, we could say that the banks, the institutions of finance capital, of course, have always been a primary target of any revolutionary organization, as well as the counterfeiting of money. Now that weed is legalized, I guess that could be done without stick-up kids and all of that stuff. We need to understand that often finance capital and the criminal enterprises of capitalism are prime targets for revolutionary movements and organizations to fund their activities.

Then, sometimes, certain activities like the after-hour clubs for the drug dealers became training exercises for newer members in the underground. Yeah, we became very good at it, in the sense that none of us or very few of us, if any, were actually captured doing this, or killed actually doing this, these expropriations. We must have been pretty good at it.

BLOOD: We were very conscious of the people who were in the bank. I don't remember anybody being shot or injured inside those banks or whatnot, because my cell, we had a saying, that we simply come in there to make a withdrawal.

DHORUBA: That's right. Unauthorized withdrawal.

BLOOD: The 9mm is our bank book.

[They laugh.]

BLOOD: . . . because that's where the money is at.

DHORUBA: Technology has changed now. We could probably do the same thing on a keyboard, with Bitcoin. We know you ain't going to do that, Blood, because you couldn't even log on.

[They laugh.]

BLOOD: Chip Fitzgerald, prior to him getting captured, the first pig he dealt with, he got shot in the back of his ear. Never went to the doctor. When they captured him, he had a little band-aid over it. He was another soldier, you know that.

DHORUBA: Like him, like Twymon, like the brother Sekou. If I had the money to write a Hollywood action movie or action drama, Sekou, I don't know who we'd get to play Sekou because Sekou would be too cool.

KALONJI: Tell us about some of those escapes with Sekou.

DHORUBA: Sekou and Twymon, man! Sekou, the reason why he went to Africa is because when they came to get him, he had his window, there was a fire escape, and they had the fire escape covered. They were outside the fire escape window, they were outside the door in the hallway. The only place to go out was out the kitchen window or something, down a drain pipe that was next to the window, and he was, like, four stories up. They had the neighborhood closed off. Sekou went down this drainpipe, through the alley, through the backyard, and the next time you heard from Sekou, he was on the telephone in Algiers.

[They laugh.]

DHORUBA: We understand that we have to do these chronicles and we have to put them down. The names just have to be changed to protect the guilty, but yeah, absolutely. That's the reason why I agreed to do this in a series. We have more comrades, like Ashanti, who I wanted to be on here too. We have other comrades who were involved at different stages and different points in the BLA and the BPP. They have extra information and insights to give to our people.

The radical history and the radical tradition of Black people is something that the enemy is now bent on trying to revise and re-market, because this mass media allows for that in a very succinct and in a very easy way.

I saw one professor who gave a thesis on the Panthers who said that, basically, she doesn't know why people have a problem with Black Lives Matter getting funding because the BPP got its money from selling books and the writings of their leaders. There's nothing further from the truth. The party raised the majority of its funds and its operational funds from selling "The Black Panther Party Newspaper" and BPP posters and stuff like that. A certain percentage a month went to the local chapter, and the rest went to the international headquarters.

I used to pick up the paper at the airport, and the enemy knew this. They said this in the COINTELPRO memos, that the BPP's major source of funds and its major means of community support came from its party community news service, its paper. That was one of the geniuses of Bobby and Huey. When we were studying revolutionary activities, Mao Zedong had said that a revolutionary organization has to have a face-to-face relationship with the masses of people. It has to have its own organ. It has to have its own voice.

That's what we did with the BPP newspaper, to the point where the paper was under constant surveillance and targeted for disruption, the paper's distributor murdered, issues stolen during transport even. Federal authorities actually used to intercept the shipments from New York, all the way. . . . They were shipping to Canada, they were shipping to Florida. When I would go to the airport, they would tell me, "Oh, that shipment is still on the plane and is going to so-and-so." This is what they did to disrupt this.

BLOOD: Let me say something about that. Dhoruba's right. One thing that the COINTELPRO did, papers coming out of California, they would set the plane down in Detroit. They would take the end strip of the paper out and put lies in there, and then ship it on the way it was going to. We read this shit on the East Coast, they said they had never heard of that shit. They were really clever in terms of how they tried to fuck us around.

DHORUBA: And how they tried to paint us into a corner in the New Left with other organizations, with white organizations that were supporting us, whether it were legal organizations or churches. People don't know, for instance, that my bail was posted by a Catholic church, and Afeni's bail was posted by Black clergy.

We need to understand that COINTELPRO went after the support network of the BPP. If people remember that book written by Dell, called *The Bonfire of the Vanities*, and stuff like that, this was partly a takeoff after Leonard Bernstein's meeting with the families and the members of the party to support the Panther 21. Leonard Bernstein was hounded and hounded into anxiety attacks by the media, because he was portrayed as a self-hating Jew who supported an antisemitic organization like the BPP.

They had a letter-writing campaign called "Dear Irving," in which a so-called member of the Communist Party was writing to their leadership complaining about Charlene Mitchell, who was a Black woman and who was in charge of Angela Davis' Defense Committee and everything, and who was running for president or the leadership in the Communist Party. She was associating with revolutionary terrorists who are antisemitic and anti-Israel. We should understand that it was our newspaper, our ability to communicate our mass line, to communicate our party line to the masses of people, masses of Black people, so that we would always be clear about what we stood for, what our community should be doing, and how we should be moving.

Of course, that's not done today with hashtag movements because you have internet gangsters, you have internet activists, internet revolutionaries, and you have hashtag movements where people never even see each other face to face hardly. Organizing these hashtag movements leaves them wide open to infiltration, to confusion and to madness, and we know that that doesn't work. It's all coming to culmination today when we see the millions of dollars that's been given to a hashtag movement, like Black Lives Matter movement or whatever you want to call it.

That money would have never gone to these people if it was #BlackLiberationMovement. If it was Black Liberation Movement, they wouldn't have got a dime. Why are you going to tell Black folks that your life matters when you know they don't give a fuck about your Black ass? You, your life will matter when they're starting coming home in body bags. When they got to deal with bodies bags, and you say, "Black Lives Matter," it'd be, "Why can't we settle this beef?" Huh? Kissinger didn't get the Nobel Peace Prize alone, he got it with Le Duc Tho who was speaking for who? He was speaking for Ho Chi Minh and the NLF and the North Vietnamese. He was speaking for people who were shooting at that time he was talking. We need to understand that white folks ain't never conquered the people, nowhere they ever went, they left voluntarily.

BLOOD: I've got to split.

JARED: Listen, first of all, brother Blood, it was an honor to meet you and to get to talk with you. Anytime you want to come back and do some more, we're happy to have you. As Dhoruba said, we intend for this to be a series.

There are so many more questions, there's so much more we want to talk with you all about. So, anytime we can provide an outlet, please let us know, or any support or any help at all, please let us know.

BLOOD: Let me say this shit to you guys, did you know the San Quentin Six? There was a brother named David Johnson. David Johnson, he's paralyzed. I just wanted to give a shout out about that. He's down in San Antonio, Texas.

JARED: I didn't know that. I need to try to get some words in. Thanks for letting us know. He contributed to our George Jackson work, on top of that too, so we appreciate him.

BLOOD: He was BGF, one of the generals.

DHORUBA: I saw him when I went out the last time. He was in the hospital when I went to see him.

BLOOD: So many of us leaving here. I'm trying to hang around. I want to live forever.

KALONJI: Stick around, brother.

DHORUBA: You're too bold to grow old, brother. You're too bold to grow old, Black.

BLOOD: You think so?

DHORUBA: We too Black to crack. Fuck these crackers.

[They laugh.]

DHORUBA: Excuse me . . . I know I'm not supposed to use that profanity. Now my fiancé looking at me like, "Oh, my God, how could you talk like that?"

BLOOD: He can delete it. He can take it out.

JARED: Nah, we going to keep it. We not sitting over here, Blood. Take it easy, Blood. Take care, Blood. Appreciate you, man.

BLOOD: Thanks again, everybody, and take care.

DHORUBA: OK, Blood, man. Is that how you exit stage-right on the cane?

[They laugh.]

DHORUBA: C'mon, you making us look bad, bro. [Laughs.]

BLOOD: I'm going to squeeze it all in. This is the best thing because when I go to the airport, and then I tell those motherfuckers to bring me a wheelchair.

[They laugh.]

DHORUBA: My man was telling me I should use that wheelchair and shit at the airport, that way I can get over.

JARED: You take off your shoes?

DHORUBA: I say, "Look, I'm seventy-six years. I ain't taking shit off." They, "OK, old man, go ahead, man."

BLOOD: About three years ago, I was there at Rio de Janeiro. I was at that airport looking at all the people. Some old fella put me in a wheelchair. I struggled to put the cane down, and every fucking thing. I'm going to tell you something, if you get a chance, go to Rio. I should have went forty years ago.

JARED: Thanks everybody. I appreciate you. Thanks everybody coming through. Shout out to everybody doing this work, and thanks everybody for making this happen. We'll catch you next time. Appreciate you, peace, everybody.

ODE TO DHORUBA BIN WAHAD

Dhoruba Bin Wahad, affectionally called "D" by those who have known him for a long time, is a gifted brotha, to say the least. He has given his entire life for the liberation of our people at home and abroad. His extraordinary analysis of "in the belly of the beast" US imperial politics and world global stage affairs is nothing short of brilliant. Whenever you want to have a better understanding of what is going on, pick up something that this brotha has written, read a position paper, listen to a recording of his, or attend one of his lectures. You will be left with clarity of purpose and understanding like never before.

Dhoruba's strength as a leader and unwavering commitment to making this world a better place will make you want to live up to being your best self. Meeting "D" shortly after graduate school, changed my life forever. I was young, curious, energetic, and wanting to make a difference in this world. I knew that Black people, poor people, and people of color were not getting their fair share. Dhoruba broke down what was happening in a way that I could understand. Not only does he explain things with such clarity, but he does it with humor thrown in! The minute you talk to him, you get the sense of how well read he is and that he knows what he is talking about regarding a multitude of issues.

I began working on his case back in the '70s and, like so many other BPP and BLA political prisoners, Dhoruba's was no different. The climate of "guilty" for anyone that dared to speak out was in the air. The FBI's COINTELPRO got many people convicted illegally and Dhoruba was one of those people.

I got to learn more from his talented team of lawyers like Bill Kunstler, Lennox Hinds, Liz Fink, Bob Bloom, and Bob Boyle—and many, many others. Everyone knew that this brilliant brotha's life was worth saving and Dhoruba began finding angles to approach his own case. Again, that is the brilliant mind of Dhoruba Bin Wahad.

Lastly, not only has he been a warrior for the people, but he has been a warrior for his most cherished role—a dad! His boys adore him and are so proud to call him their dad. To me, that's a real testament to what it's all about. All politics are local. We salute you, "D" and you will always walk with my love.

—Bibi Olugbala Angola

ABOUT THE AUTHORS

Dhoruba Bin Wahad was a leading member of the New York Black Panther Party, a Field Secretary of the BPP responsible for organizing chapters throughout the East Coast, and a member of the Panther 21. Arrested in June 1971, he was framed as part of the illegal FBI Counter Intelligence Program (COINTELPRO) and subjected to unfair treatment and torture during his nineteen years in prison. During Dhoruba's incarceration, litigation on his behalf produced over 300,000 pages of COINTELPRO documentation, and upon release in 1990 he was able to bring a successful lawsuit against the New York Department of Corrections for their criminal activities. Living in both Ghana and the US, Dhoruba continues to write and work promoting Pan-Africanism, an uncompromising critique of imperialism and capitalism, and freedom for all political prisoners.

Kalonji Jama Changa, an organizer and founder of the FTP Movement, is author of *How to Build a People's Army* and coproducer of the documentary *Organizing Is the New Cool.* Founder of Black Power Media, Changa serves as cochair of the Urban Survival and Preparedness Institute.

Joy James, Ebenezer Fitch Professor of Humanities at Williams College, is the author of *New Bones Abolition: Captive Maternal Agency and the After(life) of Erica Garner, In Pursuit of Revolutionary Love, Beyond Cop Cities,* as well as the author or editor of numerous other books and articles.

Bibi Olugbala Angola was active in many prisoner-of-war cases through the National Committee for the Defense of Political Prisoners and worked as a paralegal for Dhoruba Bin Wahad and Assata Shakur. Additionally, she worked with the National Jury Project, on the voir dire process of jury selection. She is the author of *Assata Speaks: And the People Speak on Assata* and *The Gentle Red Pen.*

ABOUT COMMON NOTIONS

Common Notions is a publishing house and programming platform that fosters new formulations of living autonomy. We aim to circulate timely reflections, clear critiques, and inspiring strategies that amplify movements for social justice.

Our publications trace a constellation of critical and visionary meditations on the organization of freedom. By any media necessary, we seek to nourish the imagination and generalize common notions about the creation of other worlds beyond state and capital. Inspired by various traditions of autonomism and liberation—in the US and internationally, historical and emerging from contemporary movements—our publications provide resources for a collective reading of struggles past, present, and to come.

Common Notions regularly collaborates with political collectives, militant authors, radical presses, and maverick designers around the world. Our political and aesthetic pursuits are dreamed and realized with Antumbra Designs.

www.commonnotions.org
info@commonnotions.org

BECOME A COMMON NOTIONS MONTHLY SUSTAINER

These are decisive times ripe with challenges and possibility, heartache, and beautiful inspiration. More than ever, we need timely reflections, clear critiques, and inspiring strategies that can help movements for social justice grow and transform society.

Help us amplify those words, deeds, and dreams that our liberation movements, and our worlds, so urgently need.

Movements are sustained by people like you, whose fugitive words, deeds, and dreams bend against the world of domination and exploitation.

For collective imagination, dedicated practices of love and study, and organized acts of freedom.
By any media necessary.
With your love and support.

Monthly sustainers start at $15 and receive each new book in our publishing program.

commonnotions.org/sustain

MORE FROM COMMON NOTIONS

New Bones Abolition: Captive Maternal Agency and the (After)life of Erica Garner
Joy James

978-1-942173-74-8
Paperback | 256 pages | 6 x 9 in | $20
Abolition | Feminism | Black Liberation

Reflecting on police violence, political movements, Black feminism, Erica Garner, Mumia Abu-Jamal, caretakers and compradors, Joy James analyzes the "Captive Maternal," which emerges from legacies of colonialism, chattel slavery and predatory policing, to explore the stages of resistance and communal rebellion that manifest through war resistance. She recognizes a long line of gendered and ungendered freedom fighters, who, within a racialized and economically-stratified democracy, transform from coerced or conflicted caretakers into builders of movements, who realize the necessity of maroon spaces, and ultimately the inevitability of becoming war resisters that mobilize against genocide and state violence.

New Bones Abolition weaves a narrative of a historically complex and engaged people seeking to quell state violence. James discusses the contributions of the mother Mamie Till-Mobley who held a 1955 open-casket funeral for her fourteen-year-old Emmett Till, murdered by white nationalists; the 1971 rebels at Attica prison; the resilience of political prisoners despite the surplus torture they endured; the emergence of Black feminists as political theorists; human rights advocates seeking abolition; and the radical intellectualism of Erica Garner, daughter of Eric Garner slain in 2014 by the NYPD. James' meditation on, and theorizing of, Black radicals and revolutionaries works to honor Agape-driven communities and organizers that deter state/police predatory violence through love, caretaking, protest, movements, marronage, and war resistance.